BARBARA

Encyclopedia
of
DOGS
and PUPPIES

(published in hardcover as *The A to Z of Dogs and Puppies*)

All you need to know about

BUYING • BREEDING • DISEASES

EXERCISING •FEEDING • HOUSE-TRAINING

INOCULATIONS • INJURIES

SHOWING • VICES

A SCARBOROUGH BOOK

STEIN AND DAY/*Publishers*/New York

PREFACE

However many books about dogs I possess, I never seem able, at the exact moment I need information, to find it quickly and easily. I therefore decided to write this book in answer to the thousands of letters I get every year from dog-owners, and to add to it the information that I feel makes the care and understanding of the dog plain to everyone. I have paid especial attention to the health of the dog and in this matter am deeply indebted to L. Guy Anderson, Esq., MRCVS, and Mrs. Patricia Cousens, MRCVS, who have so freely given me of their professional help.

Dogs bring companionship, pleasure, and profit to millions of owners, and it is the duty of every owner to learn about dogs so that he can fit them into their rightful place in the home. I want dogs to be well and truly loved and cared for "from the cradle to the grave."　　　　B.W.

SECOND SCARBOROUGH BOOKS PRINTING 1983
Encyclopedia of Dogs and Puppies
was originally published in hardcover by
Stein and Day/*Publishers*
as *The A to Z of Dogs and Puppies*.

The
A to Z
of Dogs

A TO Z OF DOGS

Abscesses. *My German Shepherd bitch keeps getting abscesses on her shoulder; what can I do for her?*

Abscesses can be caused purely and simply by bacteria, and then, of course, the cure is to administer antibiotics. Occasionally, though, abscesses are subcutaneous and are not filled with pus but with blood serum; this type clears up pretty quickly on opening. If the abscess is pus-filled, foment it frequently with hot water until the head has turned yellow. The abscess can then be punctured, the pus let out, and an antibiotic cream like aureomycin or penicillin placed on a piece of clean linen or gauze over the wound. Keep the wound open until all infection has subsided.

Antibiotics. *What are antibiotics, and what is their use to dog-owners?*

Antibiotics are chemical compounds of microbiological origin used to combat diseases caused by bacteria—they are not effective in virus infections. Antibiotics have saved many thousands of lives, human and doggy.

One of the best known is, of course, penicillin, discovered by Sir Alexander Fleming. There can be few people these days who have not at some time or other come in contact with penicillin or heard about it and its remarkable

9

power to overcome bacterial infection. It is used extensively in veterinary practice. In recent decades, many more anti-biotics have been developed, such as aureomycin and strep-tomycin, which cover a completely different range of bac-terial infections and are equally effective. Which antibiotic to use must be left to the person treating the patient. In many cases the most effective one can only be discovered by trial and error, so don't be too hard on your vet if the first treatment isn't always the successful one.

These drugs cannot be purchased without a prescription. One reason for this is that a patient can have severe re-actions to certain antibiotics. Another is that overuse kills bacteria that work for the body and thus renders the drug increasingly ineffective.

It is amazing how quickly these antibiotics can knock out a bacterial infection, and how beautifully wounds heal when one or another is applied direct to the wound. They are not only applied directly to wounds but doses are taken by mouth so that the bloodstream is supplied with them as well.

Arthritis and **Rheumatism.** *Do dogs suffer from arthritis or rheumatism?*

While arthritis is a fairly specific word, actually meaning an inflammation of a joint, rheumatism is one of those rather vague terms loosely used to cover a multitude of conditions mainly causing pain or pressure on movement. The cause of this is somewhat obscure, but it is certain that dogs are commonly affected by a condition causing muscu-lar pain, which is aggravated by movement. It most com-monly occurs in older animals and particularly when exer-cise is irregular. It sometimes occurs, for instance, in working dogs when they have a very long day that has been preceded by several days of rest. An animal that has become wet and chilled is particularly vulnerable to it.

Rheumatism may affect many different groups of muscles. It is probably most common in the muscles of the back, shoulders, and jaw, but it may be difficult to localize as almost any movement may cause distant muscles to contract. Warmth, rest, and aspirin seem to be the best first-aid methods when this condition is suspected. A mild laxative should also be given as animals frequently find it difficult to assume the position for defecation.

It is impossible to define the symptoms of arthritis because almost any joint in the body may be affected. There is usually some degree of heat and pain over the affected area, as well as lameness, if a leg is involved. Sometimes arthritis can be a very slowly developing condition and is difficult to diagnose without the use of X-ray films. It is often seen when any form of wound actually penetrates the joint capsule. The joints of the spine are particularly complex in that the vertebrae are all separated by pads, which are usually referred to as disks. Occasionally, from injury or age, or more commonly the necessary predisposition in the long-backed dog, portions of these disks protrude and interfere with the functioning of the nerves leading from the spine; some degree of paralysis varying from a slightly staggering gait to a complete paralysis follows. This condition is frequently very painful in the early stages. Treatment of these cases is rather prolonged, and considerable nursing skill may be required to assist dogs in emptying their bowels and bladders. Professional advice should be sought, and often X-ray examination is necessary to clarify diagnosis.

Barking. *I have a dog that barks incessantly at everything and nothing. He is particularly bad at night, and the neighbors are complaining. Why does he do it? How can I stop it? Am I liable legally for the nuisance to my neighbors?*

I shall take the last part of your question first. Legally you can be prosecuted if your dog is proved to be the cause of either a private or a public nuisance, but in the case of a public nuisance a private person may have to prove that that particular nuisance has caused him to suffer more than the rest of the general public. Then, too, what is a nuisance in the suburbs is not necessarily one in the depths of the country. But if a nuisance is proved, an injunction can be sought against you to prevent the continuation of the nuisance with or without a claim for damages for inconvenience caused.

I myself would seldom encourage anyone to take this kind of case to court. Going to law is a risky business—it is so easy, even when one manages to win the case, to be out of pocket over costs. A friendly approach to the owner of the dog, even a request to the police to put in a word about the nuisance, are far better plans.

In any case, matters must not be allowed to reach this stage. Persistent barking can often be cured, and I do not think it should ever be endured. A dog barks because he is bored, hysterical, or nervous; because he is spoiled and pining for affection; because he is fierce; or because he is just plain stupid. The first step must be for the owner to decide which category the dog belongs to before it is possible to diagnose the trouble and offer a solution for curing it.

The last two categories are rare, but there are, unfortunately, some dogs that are either really fierce or stupid to the point of imbecility. These are the most difficult cases of all, and in my opinion, if such dogs bark persistently, nothing can usefully be done; it is kinder to put them away.

Bored, hysterical, or nervous dogs are often those that spend the major part of their lives chained up; such dogs tend to bark to attract attention, and because their interests are so restricted, they are on edge with boredom and the slightest noise sets them off. Keeping a dog chained up like this is extremely unkind: if he is wanted as a watchdog, he can carry out that duty just as well from behind a large wire run, though even a dog penned in like this should be taken out and given a long run at least once a day. Plenty of exercise is really the answer, for a tired dog will not bark. Apart from exercise it also helps for this type of dog to mix a lot with human beings and occasionally also with other dogs; they become much more placid when they have been taken out and about.

The type of dog that causes most trouble is the spoiled one belonging to an oversentimental owner. Some cases follow a long spell of serious illness when the owner is, sympathetically but quite mistakenly, doing everything he can to "make it up to the dog for all it has suffered." Dogs don't understand that kind of thing; they simply put it down to softness on the part of the owner. They lose all respect for him and consider they can play him up whenever they feel like it. Instead of lying quietly in their beds as they are told when the owner leaves the room at night, they bark and whine and make everybody's life a misery. It is your duty to stop this noise today. Whenever the dog barks in the course of the day, you should give him a really good shaking on the choke chain and tell him, in a voice that is unrelenting and authoritative, to lie down. If he is then good and quiet, you must be sure to praise him generously. At night, by showing both firmness and love, you must get the dog to lie quietly in his basket when you leave the room and, should he either get up or bark, you must rush back *just once* and scold him really fiercely. You must sound very angry, and once you have left the room for the second time, you must not come back, however much the dog may bark or whine.

Oversentimental owners often fail in this treatment. They find it difficult to get a sufficiently stern note into their voice, and they also keep asking themselves: "Can there be something wrong with him? Should I go back to make sure?" when they ought to harden their hearts against the frustrated dog's barking. In such cases the help of a professional trainer should be sought. Some owners think trainers maltreat dogs; what trainers do is simply to make the dog understand, where the owner seems incapable of doing this, that no nonsense will be tolerated. Formerly, when I ran a residential training school for dogs and owners, the dogs were put to bed in kennels built into the rooms. The owner would put the dog to bed but was not allowed to return to the dog if he barked. I used to go once to the room to scold the dog and then to comfort him, after which he was left to his own devices. The dog found the scolding unpleasant; he also found that making a noise didn't bring the owner back. It sometimes took two days for the lesson to sink in, but we always won in the end.

Most people imagine they are being very firm with their dogs and are really surprised when I tell them that both their voices and their attitude to their dogs are rather more like blancmange than anything else. I am never angry; I just put on an act. Dogs understand.

Bathing. *How often should I bathe my dog? Can I let him bathe in the sea?*

There is no hard and fast rule as to how often to bathe a dog. If your dog smells or is scratching, or is losing his coat excessively, I should bathe him. If his coat is clean and shiny and you groom him regularly, I think he shouldn't be bathed more than once every three months. Bathing softens the coat and takes away natural oil, although the friction from rubbing the dog dry and getting out the old coat more than makes up for these things. Always use a good dog soap,* and the result should be a nice sweet-smelling, clean dog.

Bathing in the sea is not good for dogs' coats and often leads to eczema. Let him bathe if he wishes, but pop him into the bath afterward, and rinse the salt out with warm water before drying him. Otherwise the salt leaves a deposit

---

*The author uses tetmosol, which is not available in the United States. It has pesticidal and fungicidal properties.

in the coat, which eventually leads to scratching. Long-coated breeds suffer from this more than short-coated ones. If you want proof that sea water is bad for hair, see what a state your own hair is in after a few days of swimming in the briny.

Bitches in Heat. *How can I protect my bitch from unwanted visiting dogs while she is in heat?*

Nowadays the use of chlorophyll in large doses has been found to be extremely effective in preventing male dogs from picking up the strong scent emitted by a bitch in heat, and I have also proved with my own bitches that by commencing dosing according to the directions with clorophyll, they can be taken out comfortably without being molested by dogs. Some people even take them to shows—with the exception of obedience shows, which are barred to bitches in heat by Kennel Club rules—and the dogs completely ignore the bitches' presence. I have run residential dog-training courses at my home with male dogs in the house and my own two bitches in heat, and no male dog fussed or made any attempt to get near my bitches when they were dosed as mentioned. But I do think one is taking an unnecessary risk if one does not closely confine the bitches for the last five days of the heat period—the bitches themselves are extremely provocative toward any dog at this vital stage and do everything in their power to attract the male dog.

The quantity of chlorophyll to be given depends entirely on the size and weight of the dog. Directions are enclosed, and the owner of each dog must work out what that particular dog needs. The substance is quite harmless, so no one need be frightened of giving an overdose.

It is always helpful to wash the bitch's vulva two or three times a day with a chlorophyll solution. If possible, exercise her away from your own premises. I usually take my bitches in the car some distance away before letting them run; thus if there were any scent to be picked up, it would not lead the male dogs to my house.

Most people want to know when to start dosing their bitches with chlorophyll. The answer is: as soon as you notice the swelling of the bitch's vulva and discharge of blood from the genital passage. The period of heat varies vastly in bitches, but nine to fifteen days is about average. Some bitches come in heat only once a year, some as many as four times a year; the greatest number do so twice a year. The bitch is ready for mating as the discharge lessens and she stands with her tail turned sideways. This is the time when, whether you are using chlorophyll or not, I recommend careful isolation from any male dog.

Bitches in Whelp. *I am going to breed my little Poodle bitch for the first time. I am very ignorant of what goes on after mating, and am most interested in the stages of growth from conception to birth. Should I give her any help at whelping time?*

This is a very big subject, but I will try to tell you very concisely what you want to know.

At the time of mating, the egg cells, or ova as they are called, leave the bitch's ovary and find their way into the fallopian tube. The male spermatozoa move up through the womb, or uterus, into the fallopian tube, where they fuse with the female ova. These then start to divide and after a few days reach the uterus, where they burrow into the thickened lining membrane. They go on dividing and form the chorion, or caul. This protects the puppies during pregnancy and also nourishes them. This nourishing part is known as the placenta; here the interchange of food, oxygen, and waste products occurs between puppies and their dam. But the two blood systems are divided by a thin membrane so that the mother and her puppies have separate blood supplies. Meanwhile the cells of the ova are developing into the puppies you will eventually know.

I will give you roughly the rate of growth of the fetus.

At 10 days the ova are approximately 1/12 to 1/20 inch long.

At 3-4 weeks old they are approximately 1 inch in length.

At 6 weeks old they are approximately 3½ inches long.

At 7-8 weeks old they are approximately 5 inches long.

At the 9th week they are 6-8 inches long.

The stages of development are interesting as well.

At 10 days the fertilized ova have reached the uterus.

At 10-21 days traces of the fetus appear, and traces of head, body, and limbs can be discerned.

At 3-4 weeks the first indications of claws can be seen.

At the 5th week the stomach is well defined. At 6 weeks large hairs appear on lips, eyelids, etc.

At 7-8 weeks the eyelashes have appeared, and hair is beginning to appear at the tip of the tail, head, and extremities.

By the 9th week the puppy is getting fully covered with hair and ready for its birth.

The average bitch carries her litter for from 58 to 63 days, although it has been known for puppies to have been carried 70 days. Before 58 days the puppies are unlikely to be alive.

Milk should be a part of the bitch's diet and, if she likes it, occasionally fish and an egg. A varied diet at this time helps to provide all the vitamins necessary for healthy growth. As whelping time approaches, the bitch will become restless, she will have milk, and she will try to make a bed for herself. I have always found that if there is a nice warm cupboard in the kitchen or living room, bitches love to choose this for the birth of their litter. I usually put plenty of newspapers on the floor and then an old blanket.

The puppies are each born separately in their fetal membranes, but these should have ruptured when the puppy is born. If this does not happen, they must be immediately ruptured by the owner; the afterbirth follows each birth. The navel string is usually bitten through by the mother; if this doesn't happen, it must be cut. Normally, however, the owner need do nothing except watch the bitch to make sure she doesn't savage her puppies. If she looks as though she is going to do this, remove the puppies as they are born and place them in a hot blanket kept warm by a heating pad or hot-water bottle. Then return them to the mother after the last one is born. Make sure she has milk for them by squeezing the nipples, and then leave her to suckle them in peace. When she has settled down, and had a drink of warm milk and a little ground beef, you can change the soiled newspaper and blanket and make all clean and tidy.

The only time to really worry is if the bitch strains and strains and no puppy appears. If this is happening and the delay is unduly long between births, it may mean a dead or deformed puppy, and veterinary aid should be called. The other time to worry is if no births are occurring and a bloody or green discharge appears. Most owners suffer more than the bitch and keep an eye on the clock, wondering whether in fact they ought to call assistance. Only experience will instruct an owner, but most animals are best left to their own devices.

Biting, Indiscriminate. *What shall I do? My dog bites me every time I take anything away from him or give him a command. He even bites me when I caress him, yet he is only ten months old. Nor is it only me he bites; all the tradesmen are terrified of him.*

I gather from your query that you have only recently decided that this biting is not puppy play. So many owners let this habit grow until the dog is master of the situation! It is oversentimental owners who produce biting dogs, and few of these on their own, even with instruction, can cure this vice. They need expert help, for the cure is to return violence with violence.

If you are going to attempt to cure him yourself, suspend him off his front legs by his choke chain as he is about to bite, and scold him in a violent tone of voice; do not put him back on his front legs until he shows signs of discomfort (usually after about ten seconds). Now he will be subdued; caress and praise him. Repeat this process every time he persists in the habit; you will certainly have to do so several times if the vice is deeply ingrained. A dog despises you if he bites you; force him to respect you. I know it sounds cruel, but it is not, and it is much kinder than death in the gas chamber, to which further biting may well lead. Until he is really cured, make sure he gets no opportunities to attack tradesmen and, in any case, take out an insurance policy so that you will not be out of pocket if he should bite someone.

Biting, Pseudoprotective. *I have a German Shepherd that attacks everyone who approaches me, yet is perfectly sweet when I am not about. I like to know I am safe when out with my dog but fear he will bite someone. What shall I do?*

This is a trait that many dogs have, especially German Shepherds and Corgis. It is part of their shepherding instinct and, if not checked young, is quite incurable. The owners enjoy it at first instead of severely scolding their dogs, and by the time the dog is about eighteen months old, it is difficult to stop. Taking the dog, muzzled if necessary, among crowds is one of the best ways to cure this habit. Get people to touch him (muzzled), and give him a terrific scolding if he attempts to attack. If this fails, get someone who trains dogs to snatch him from you and really shake him when he shows signs of being vicious. He must be defeated, then praised.

Boarding Kennels. *I hear such awful tales of people leaving their dogs in boarding kennels and finding them thin and in bad coat when they return. How can I find somewhere where my dog will receive really good attention?*

If you cannot take your dog on holiday, he must of course be boarded, though I hope this is not being done because the dog is not well behaved enough to be taken with you. If that is the case, do start training it to lie down and stay down alone each day, as many motels and some hotels allow well-behaved dogs in their owners' rooms.

American Automobile Association regional tourbooks give all the motels and hotels approved by the AAA that accept pets. There may be a charge for this. However, if you are going abroad, you must of course find a suitable home for your dog.

If you can find someone who has boarded their dog out in satisfactory kennels, a personal knowledge of these holiday homes is by far the best recommendation. Otherwise, your veterinarian may be able to suggest a kennel, or you may find kennels advertised in local newspapers, in *Dog World*, or in other dog-fanciers' magazines. You can always inspect the kennel before committing your pet to it.

Some people, while they are on holiday, send their dogs away to be trained. I do not recommend this because it is the owner that really needs the training. Not only that, but the dog's affection will be given to the trainer and if he has been kindly handled, he may fret when he is separated from the trainer. There is a risk, too, of the dog's getting a disease or escaping without the owner there to help care for him.

I run weekend courses for dogs and owners who attend daily; those from a distance stay with their dogs in local hotels. The dogs are fully trained in seven hours' working time. We work from 10:00 A.M. to 3:00 P.M., breaking for lunch at 12:30 until 2:00 P.M. We spend a lot of time with the dogs and owners out in the fields, teaching the dogs to come when called.

Breeding, Practical. *I have arranged to take my bitch to be mated during her next heat. Can you tell me anything I ought to know?*

Having chosen your male sire for the future litter by pedigree, by seeing his offspring, and by noting the qualities you wish impressed on the offspring—above all his masculinity and temperament—you will have the job of seeing if your bitch likes the chosen mate. For some bitches are distinctly shy breeders and absolutely refuse to have anything to do with the dog chosen for them. This can be extremely annoying. Nowadays artificial insemination is used in rare cases and no doubt will be used more and more in the future, but unless such facilities are available, natural mating is still essential. If the bitch is determined to have nothing to do with the dog of the owner's choice, she may have to be allowed the last word in the matter of choosing a sire. One can sometimes hold the bitch in position for the dog if she is really ready to be mated—which one can test by taking her near the dog, when she will stand provocatively with her tail flat to her side—but I feel this is a bad thing and might cause injury to the bitch. Always let her play with the dog first, if possible somewhere where they can be alone but watched. She may be coy at first and then suddenly decide to acquiesce.

Sometimes difference of height makes mating difficult. Breeders use raised ground to counteract this or even a box for a small dog to stand on. This mating of difficult cases should really be left to experienced breeders; the average owner need only take the bitch along to the stud dog and call back for it. Some novices have been frightened at the length of time the dog and bitch are joined together, but this is a perfectly normal thing and calls for no interference.

Some people prefer to mate a bitch twice, and of course if the bitch were left with the dog, they would mate many times, but this is not a good thing. For one thing you do not want too big a litter, especially for a young maiden bitch.

Occasionally a terrible-looking puppy is born and the owner of the bitch runs cursing to the owner of the stud dog, but it may simply be a throwback, or atavism as it is called, and nobody can tell which side has this hereditary tendency. In such cases it is of course wiser not to use the same stud dog again. If the same thing happens again with a litter fathered by another sire, it is obviously the bitch's fault, and she is not one to use for breeding purposes. In cases where a mating does not induce pregnancy, the usual thing is for the bitch to be entitled to one free remating.

The bitch stays in heat anything up to twenty-one days, but for the first seven days she is passing a bloodstained discharge and will not allow male dogs near her. After the discharge ceases, she will usually be ready to mate on about the ninth to the fifteenth day, but there are variations on either side of these dates.

Sterility can be due to a number of things. Lack of estrus, or heat as it is called, is a common cause. Bitches usually come in heat for the first time between six and nine months, and most commonly in spring and autumn, but nowadays under artificial conditions bitches show estrus at any time of the year. Then again twice annually is the usual thing, but some of the small breeds come in heat only once a year.

Sterility can be caused by the absence of ova, or by stunted growth that affects the genital organs. It may also be due to nymphomania, which causes the bitch to be almost continually in heat and which is in most cases due to chronic inflammation of the ovary; sometimes it is even caused by cysts. Only an examination by a vet can help in these cases. The lack of vitamin E has been found to cause sterility, as has excessive fat. Too much inbreeding causes weakness of the strain and is a contributory factor to sterility.

A lot of sterility is caused by the male dog; the absence of sperm, a deficiency of semen, and excess fat are all causes, and examination of the semen under a microscope will determine if lack of live spermatozoa is the cause. Naturally any disease in either male or female may also result in temporary, if not permanent, sterility.

Nowadays the judicious use of hormone products helps to reduce sterility. While we are on this subject, should a bitch in heat escape and be accidentally mated, heat can be brought on again by Stilboestrol given by the vet and the pregnancy terminated. This however must be done quickly.

Finally there are some general remarks for owners of bitches. Never breed a bitch at her first heat, but wait for the second. Never breed unless you want to do so for pleasure or profit. There still goes around the old wives' tale that if you don't breed a bitch, she will get ill and her uterus will get diseased. This is nonsense: pyometra (pus in the womb) happens just as often in bitches that have had puppies as with those that have not, probably more. The other fallacy is that to breed a bitch stops her having false pregnancies or pseudopregnancies as they are called. This is not so. I once owned a bitch that had had six litters, and she had such realistic false pregnancies that I really began to wonder whether she had somehow got away and got mated. She had every symptom of pregnancy, and all the drugs that the vet prescribed did no good at all. During each false pregnancy she tore up my sofa and anything else she could get hold of; this was her pathetic method of making a nest.

Breeding, Theoretical. *I am thinking of taking up breeding but am not at present quite clear about the meaning of such terms as linebreeding and inbreeding. What exactly are they, and what points generally should be kept in mind when choosing sire and dam for breeding?*

If you are going to take up dog breeding seriously, you must read books on the subject; you must attend shows, and study heredity, breeding for certain qualities, linebreeding, and inbreeding. First of all, you must realize what you are aiming at. People imagine that if they buy a bitch with

"Champion" written all over her pedigree, they are certain to have a perfect dam to start breeding with. All they have to do, they think, is find the equally marvelous sire with "Champion" all over his pedigree, and the resulting litter will be perfect. How wrong they are! To get the perfect puppy, let alone the perfect litter, often takes experienced breeders a lifetime of trial and error, and will hardly ever be achieved at the first attempt.

We know the old saying "Like begets like," but what we may not know is what characteristics past generations have passed on to dam and sire. Such characteristics may not be discernible in the parents-to-be, yet a mating could produce something vastly different from what we expected. Only by having litters can one prove what that particular mating will produce. Always remember that dam and sire exert equal influence on the litter, and it may therefore be unfair to blame the sire for the faults of the offspring. Choose your bitch just as carefully as you choose your sire, and remember temperament. This is most important. However good the puppies, if they are nervous or fierce, they will not be welcomed either as pets or for show purposes. Both sides should be chosen for the greatest number of desirable qualities in each and for their ability to stamp these qualities on their offspring. Therefore, if possible, see stock that the sire has fathered, and note any good or bad points. The mating together of two animals with the same good or bad points tends to fix these points and, in the case of the bad ones, they are almost sure to be passed on by the offspring when they breed in turn.

This brings me to inbreeding, which is of course the mating together of closely related dogs and is done in the hope of stamping certain good qualities in those dogs on their offspring. Linebreeding is simply choosing dogs from the same line of descent to be mated together with the object of accumulating blood on both sides that you particularly like in your breed of dog.

The most dangerous method to dabble in is inbreeding, as the mated dogs have practically the same ancestors and you may therefore again find that not only have the good points you hoped to stamp on the progeny become fixed but also some of the faults. This is often the case when the matings are arranged more on the basis of studying the pedigrees than the two dogs themselves. No dog with any bad feature at all should be mated with another bearing the same feature. Inbreeding fixes characteristics, and with sensible selection very superior progeny can be produced, though very often this improvement is only noted in one or two of the litter. Inbreeding is not a 100 percent method of getting what you want in all the puppies—very far from it—but it is the shortest known cut to stamping a family likeness on the litters you breed. Unfortunately it often leads to a deterioration of constitution, size, and temperament, and what you gain upon the swings you may lose upon the roundabouts.

Inbreeding is not an unnatural phenomenon. Formerly, when dogs ran wild in packs, the most powerful male was the sire of all the puppies in the pack, and that of course led to intensive inbreeding. But what we are inclined to forget is that in those days the survival of the fittest was the rule, and the weaklings never survived. In these days of specialized dog-breeding, when puppies mean money, the weakest in the litter may be hand-reared, which is of course a very bad thing for the race.

Not all inbreeding is harmful, or sure to make the strain lose vigor or produce bad temperament. These faults occur also with matings between completely unrelated animals, and one is far more likely to know what one is going to get as the result of inbreeding than by indiscriminate breeding from an unknown, unrelated sire. If the same constitutional weakness appears in both sides of the parents to be inbred, then undoubtedly that weakness will be stamped in a terrifying way on the progeny. If, however, the breeder inbreeds sensibly by choosing only vigorous, fertile parents, rejecting all signs of any weakness, the resulting puppies should have indelibly stamped on them the good qualities sought after. I do not feel it is wise for amateur breeders to indulge in this method of breeding. It depends entirely on the skill used in selecting the dogs to be mated.

Linebreeding is an entirely different process, and some of the best dogs in the world owe their beauty, temperament, and vigor to being linebred for generations. This is of course done chiefly on pedigree as well as selection, but you do not stamp the particular quality you require so quickly on the progeny as you do with inbreeding.

Breed Standards. *I want to breed my Bloodhound bitch and to exhibit the best of the progeny at the principal shows. Where can I find out what constitutes an ideal Bloodhound? Who can tell me what characteristics are considered faults?*

A clearly defined set of standards (and in the case of some breeds, a list of faults) is laid down in respect of each of the 116 breeds at present recognized by the American Kennel Club as eligible for show competition. These standards are published in The American Kennel Club's *Complete Dog Book* (Doubleday, 1969). The standards laid down for a perfect Bloodhound, for instance, would include characteristics, general appearance, head and skull, eyes, ears, neck, forequarters, body, hindquarters, feet, tail, color, and weight and size. This book will be found to contain much of interest to the dog-owner who is just beginning in the show world.

Buying a Dog. *I want to buy a dog. Can you give me any hints that will help me get a nice one? How am I protected in law from fraudulent sellers of puppies? I am a complete novice in this dog-buying business.*

Do you want a pure-bred animal? In that case, seek

advice from someone who knows about dogs; read as much as possible about the breed you fancy; go to shows, pick the breeders' brains, and watch the type of dog that wins prizes. If you want a mongrel, it is easier to buy a puppy without fear of being cheated, but you will never have quite the same pride in possessing a crossbred as you would in owning a pedigreed animal. What you will finally buy will depend on your purse, but whatever the type of dog, choose a strong puppy; one that has clear, big eyes; a damp, cold nose; and is active and friendly both with other puppies and with human beings. Make sure the parents, or parent if only the mother can be seen, are not shy creatures.

If you want to buy a dog and have the complete remedy in law for any breach of warranty, the seller must be told exactly what you want and must warrant either by word or in writing that the puppy that is being sold to you has the desired requirements. It is always assumed in law that the seller has the right to sell that particular dog. A warranty doesn't cover an obvious defect. If a person is silly enough to buy a dog with no tail when that breed should have one, no warranty that the animal was pure-bred would make a claim valid purely on the grounds of that dog having no tail as it should have had. If a pedigree is given with the puppy, that pedigree is supposed to be a true one belonging to that particular puppy. If the buyer can prove that that is not so, there will be a case for claiming damages from the seller. The buyer should, immediately he finds out, inform the seller he is returning the purchase or, if he prefers, retain the animal and sue for damages. The seller's action comes under fraud, which is different from a breach of warranty. I recommend that expert advice be taken in all these matters of law. However right one feels, and however clear the case seems, the law is never as simple as it appears.

You should be able to make an arrangement with the seller so that you can get your vet to look the puppy over for you, and can be thoroughly satisfied before you clinch the deal.

The American Kennel Club gives the following advice to buyers of AKC registrable dogs:

When you buy a dog that is represented as being eligible for registration with The American Kennel Club, you are entitled to receive an AKC application form properly filled out by the seller, which, when completed by you and submitted to AKC with the proper fee, will enable you to effect the registration of the dog. When the application has been processed in this office, you will receive an AKC registration certificate.

Under AKC rules, any person who sells dogs that he represents as AKC registrable, must maintain records that will make it possible for him to give full identifying information with every dog he delivers, even though AKC papers may not yet be available. Do not accept a promise of later identification.

The Rules and Regulations of The American Kennel Club stipulate that whenever someone sells or delivers a dog that he says may be registered with AKC, he must identify the dog either by putting into the hands of the buyer a properly completed AKC registration application or by giving the buyer a bill of sale or a written statement, *signed by the seller*, giving the dog's full breeding information as follows:

Breed, sex, and color of the dog
Date of birth of the dog
Registered names of the dog's sire and dam
Name of its breeder

Persons who purchase dogs that are represented as being eligible for registration with The American Kennel Club and who encounter problems in acquiring the necessary registration application forms should write to The American Kennel Club, 51 Madison Avenue, New York, New York 10010, giving all of the information they received at the time of purchase. The AKC will attempt to assist them in the matter.

I am sorry to have to say that few strays seem to be satisfactory pets; they have tasted wild, uncontrolled living and do not settle down very easily. I deal with a lot of desperate owners whose kind hearts have gone out to strays, and often they have brought trouble. Naturally it works out in some cases, but the owner must be a good one, willing to train the stray in good behavior.

I am not, in this book, going into details of the various breeds; there are more than a hundred of these, all charming and fascinating in their own way. If you have time to spare, buy a dog that keeps you busy combing and titivating him up; if you are overworked, buy a short-haired dog. If you have suitable premises, buy a big dog; if you have a one-room apartment, buy a tiny dog. Whatever dog you buy will be the best in the world, for it will be your dog.

Canned Meat. *I am the owner of a Spaniel puppy, three months old. I go to work during the day, and my aged mother looks after her for me. I have little time for shopping to buy the puppy raw meat. Is canned dog meat as good?*

For years people said dogs could eat and thrive on anything, including butchers' waste offal, scraps from the table. No doubt, some could. For those who could afford it when meat was cheap, fresh butchers' meat provided the ideal food for dogs. But science has progressed, and with it have come advanced and perfected methods of canning all fresh food. We live to a much greater extent on canned and frozen foods than was ever dreamed of by our grandparents. Why, therefore, should not dogs benefit by the knowledge that science has gained and have good canned dog meat? It is pressure-cooked to conserve all the goodness, juices, and vitamins, remaining fresh indefinitely while unopened.

Recently I was asked by a processor of dogfood to test out on my own dogs and the dogs that attend my training school a "meat-and-liver" canned dogfood. I sent dozens of cans to breeders rearing tiny puppies from three weeks old and asked them to test it out on these puppies by dividing the litters in half and weighing each group. The half not fed on this canned meat was fed on shin of beef and puppy meal; both groups had milk of course.

The results were eminently satisfactory. The gain in weight was slightly more in those fed on the canned meat than the control group. They suffered no digestive upsets and were bright and energetic, and their growth was normal. The dams were fed on the same canned meat. The kennels testing this had Poodles and Corgis. I then switched to German Shepherds and Miniature Black-and-Tan Terriers. The results were the same.

Next I asked sixty members of my training club to test it for a week on every imaginable type and breed of dog and to report to me whether they found it good, bad, or indifferent. All said the dogs ate it with great relish, including those who previously were dainty over their food.

All were fit and well, and had no digestive upsets.

Thus I conclude from these experiments and from feeding my own valuable dogs on it, and those that stay at my residential school, that, in this case at any rate, canned dog meat can be equal to, and probably much superior to, raw meat of various qualities. It is easy to store, as it keeps indefinitely. It is all meat and liver, and great quantities are not needed to satisfy a dog. It compares favorably in price with fresh meat of excellent quality. Therefore from personal experience I can say your puppy would be well fed on a good brand of canned meat for dogs.

Car Journeys. *I would like to take my dog everywhere with me in the car, but he is such a nuisance. He barks at passersby when the car is stationary; when I am driving, he puts hiw paws on my shoulders, and I feel he might easily cause me to have an accident. How does one keep a dog lying down in the back where he belongs?*

It certainly is extremely unwise to have a dog rampaging about while you are driving your car. Until he has learned to lie down and stay down on your command, he should be tied safely in the back. A cord tied to the two window handles and a very short cord attached to his collar and then connected to the one between the windows makes it impossible for him to move any distance. Should he make a noise or try to jump about, stop the car and turn round and force him into the down position by pulling on his choke chain and giving firm commands to lie down. Be really angry if he gets up. Try to get a friend to help you with this; he can make the dog lie down while you are driving very slowly. Otherwise it means that you have to keep stopping, which is very annoying. If he really won't stop barking, you may have to muzzle him temporarily. I have got owners to put a staple in the floor of the car and run a long lead attached to the dog's collar from the collar down to the floor and through the staple. A friend holds the end of the lead and, if the dog attempts to get up, he can be pulled down again. The tension on the lead is released or tightened as he behaves or misbehaves.

Care of the Litter. *My Boxer bitch is due to whelp any day now. Can you give me some advice on the care of the puppies?*

During the first three weeks the mother will do everything necessary for the care of the puppies. Incidentally, do not worry too much if she kicks one particular puppy out of the nest. Inexperienced owners keep putting it back, or even try rearing it on a bottle. I have always found, if I have done this, that there is something wrong with the puppy. The mother seems to know; therefore unless it is an extremely valuable one, I strongly advise that this one should be put away.

Start weaning the puppies at about three weeks old. Teach them to drink warm milk by putting a drop on the end of their muzzles; they will lick it off. Teach them to eat tiny morsels of ground beef by placing little pieces on the very tip of their tongues. In no time at all the puppies will be eager for this extra food, and the bitch will move away from them quite a lot. By six weeks old they should be weaned, although some people like to give them another week or two. In nice weather they should be allowed to play in the sun on the lawn or a rug. That is why puppies born in the summer are so much easier to raise than winter-born puppies.

The puppies should be wormed at three months and again at six months; after that they should be all right.

Puppies should have extra vitamins given to them, plenty of good food and fresh air, not forgetting warm, dry, and draftproof sleeping quarters. They should never get over-tired by being mauled by children. It makes them irritable, and they start to growl or snap at an early age. Handle them by all means, but watch for the signal of the growl or wriggling away that shows they have had enough.

Teach them from the earliest days to be housebroken; this is achieved by popping them out every two hours to the same spot with the same words, "Hurry up," and giving plenty of praise when they perform. A watchful owner seldom has a dirty puppy for long. Never teach them on newspaper—a filthy habit if ever there was one. If they must perform in a flat, give them a tray of sand or turf. Association of ideas is everything, and no one wants a dog in later life to associate paper with relieving itself. Start the way you mean to go on.

Castration. *My dog is most embarrassing in the house; he pretends to have sexual play with cushions or the children's legs. My walks are a nightmare, as I am dragged to every lamppost. Can I give pills or something to make my dog less sexy?*

Yes, there are hormone preparations that can be given to help this, but I have found them pretty useless, and in some cases have actually known them to make the dog worse. The best thing to do, if the dog is not wanted for showing, is to get the vet to castrate it.

I know of no ill effects after this operation and cannot

imagine why more dogs are not operated on. They do not lose their character nor, with judicious feeding, do they become fat. They are gay, happy dogs and much nicer to own. That is more than I can say for bitches that have been spayed (had their ovaries removed). They become dull and lazy, and run to fat very easily as they get older.

Of castration, a veterinary surgeon writes:

This operation is comparatively simple and consists of the surgical removal of both testicles. This, of course, necessitates a general anesthetic, but with modern methods of anesthesia and a healthy animal, that presents very little risk. Each testicle is then removed by making an incision in the scrotal sac, ligating the spermatic cord and excising the organ. The wound is left to drain and is not sutured; healing takes place very rapidly, being complete in seven days. Within a fortnight the adult animal is completely recovered, and is ready to resume training.

The result of this operation becomes apparent during the ensuing months. The animal no longer shows any sexual excitement in the presence of other dogs or bitches, becomes more tractable, and responds more readily to training, without losing any of his joie de vivre. Of course the loss of his sexual interest results in a greater interest in food and comfort. The animal is more eager for his meals and readily clears up much more than he actually requires. Owners should not succumb to the temptation of overfeeding, as there is a tendency for the animal to put on weight. Excessive weight is very hard to reduce once it has been allowed to develop.

In conclusion, should an owner be advised to consider this operation as a solution to some training problem, he need have no hesitation in deciding to have his dog castrated. Indeed, there is no reason why dogs in general should not be subjected to this operation as puppies, particularly if they are required as companions for children or old people, or in the case of mongrels which are of no use for breeding. The dog is one of the few domestic animals in this country which is not neutered as a routine unless required for stud purposes. It is to be hoped that the idea may be adopted more readily in the future, resulting in happier, more contented dogs.

Chasing Cars. *My dog chases cars. How can I stop him?*

I know you don't want the answer: Why allow the dog the freedom of the road where he can chase cars? For that is of course not a cure but an expedient. The cure is to give the dog such a fright when he goes into the attack that he never chases one again. I have known many methods tried. I have known someone who sat on the hood of a car with a riding crop and, as the dog came in to bite the wheels, gave it an almighty smack with the whip. That stopped that dog forever. I have heard of jugs of water being poured over the dog, of hard objects being aimed at the dog, and of course there is always the old method of the long cord and the jerk when he attacks the car, and the subsequent punishment of the dog. But the cause of the dog's behavior is always the same: lack of obedience training. If a dog came when called, he would not chase anything.

Nearly all vice in dogs is caused by lack of training when young, by the owners having too little time to spare for the dog when that dog is at the impressionable age when training is easy. Familiarity breeds contempt, and it is far more sensible to take a dog when quite young into a busy town and accustom him to traffic so that the excitement of chasing it never arises. The owner must not be soft when a dog on lead tries to chase a car. A severe jerk and a good shaking work wonders, providing the owner's voice sounds really furious. A weak-voiced owner is useless when it comes to correcting a dog.

Choke Chains. *I have been advised by my local training club to use a choke chain on my dog. It sounds terribly cruel to me, yet my dog pulls my arms out, and I must do something. What is your opinion of choke chains?*

So many people imagine that choke chains are used to hurt a dog when, in fact, their purpose is exactly the opposite, namely, to make it possible to correct the dog firmly without in any way causing hurt or damage. Choke chains—and I mean the thick-linked variety—are far kinder than leather collars would be, and the only feeling the dog experiences is surprise at being checked.

If your choke chain does not seem to achieve its purpose, you are not jerking hard enough. This may be due to false sentiment or, in the case of a large dog, lack of strength. If the former, put sentiment aside; if the latter, get the strong man of the family to do the jerks. No dog will pull after two minutes of the right jerks.

Personally I insist on all dogs, even tiny toys, wearing thick-lined choke chains for training purposes. If you are still in doubt, get my 16mm film *"Love Me, Love My Dog."** It will prove to you that I pull really hard without hurting or depressing the dog. The sooner the general public realize why and how experienced dog-lovers use choke chains, the better their dog-training will be.

Cysts, Interdigital. *My dog has lumps between his toes in summer. I am told by local know-alls that they are caused by grass seeds, yet I don't walk the dog where there are any grass seeds. What are they?*

There are many different opinions as to what causes these interdigital cysts. I think most people agree that somehow organisms have entered the tissues where these suppurating swellings appear, and caused hard painful lumps, which the dogs lick and lick. They burst and heal up and then, very often, break out again. They often clear up after incision and treatment with some antibiotic. With my own dog aureomycin has worked like magic, but most vets have their own ideas on the best treatment for each individual case. Hot fomentations are extremely good and can very often prevent surgery.

*You can rent this from the Royal Society for the Prevention of Accidents, 17 Knightsbridge, London, S.W. 1.

Dogs that get out of condition are more likely to get these cysts, and I have found a course of vitamins an enormous help in preventing their appearance. I am positive that walking on newly tarred or concrete surfaces is a major cause of trouble, and I do not think grass seeds a likely explanation.

Cystitis. *My bitch seems to try to pass water very often with no effective result. What is the matter with her?*

She may have cystitis, or inflammation of the bladder, which is usually caused by a chill. She will cry out when her bladder is pressed and may also cry out when she passes urine. This trouble is usually knocked out by antibiotics. This complaint is not to be confused with cysts or tumors.

Destructiveness. *My house is wrecked daily by my dog. It seems to do it for sheer devilment because it leaves its bones and toys alone. What can I do?*

Idle dogs and idle people always get into trouble. Train the dog—give it something to think about, and to tire it out. Then make an indoor kennel where it can be shut in when you are not there to watch it. If you must leave it free until cured, you could make it wear a Greyhound-type muzzle; it would soon get used to it just as Greyhounds do. Male dogs do this wrecking as a form of masturbation; castration is the cure for that.

Naturally you must scold your dog and show him what he has done wrong. It is useless reasoning with a dog, as some oversentimental people tell me they have done. Dogs are not clever enough to be reasoned with. They must understand they are really naughty and you are extremely angry with them. If the tearing up still continues, the dog must have a safe kennel outside where he may lose the habit and be able to return to the house.

Dewclaws. *I understand that puppies should have their dewclaws removed. When and how ought this to be done?*

In my opinion, dewclaws should be taken off at the same time as docking is done and, even if the dog is never docked, its dewclaws should be removed at a few days old for its health and safety, and the safety of its owner. Dewclaws can grow inward and cause the dog intense pain, or they can tear clothes as the dog jumps. They are of no practical use to the dog. Some breeds, however, like Great Pyrenees, have double dewclaws and these are part and parcel of the breed standard* and must be kept intact—why, I utterly fail to understand. But then there is a lot in the doggy world I fail to understand!

The removal of dewclaws can be done very easily with a sharp pair of surgical scissors—the kind that curve outward. The claws are cut off as near the leg as is practical without injuring the skin. Tincture of benzoin compound is applied to the incision; nothing more need be done. In my opinion, it is better to remove both front and back dewclaws, as I have seen dogs with nasty leg wounds where the dewclaws have caught in something and torn away.

Diabetes. *My eight-year-old dog suddenly seems to be drinking a lot of water and is consequently passing what seems to me to be an excessive amount of urine. He is thin, yet his tummy seems bloated. What do you think is the matter with him?*

Naturally it is very difficult to answer this without seeing the dog, but it sounds like diabetes to me. The first thing to do is to have his urine tested for sugar. Diabetes is a condition in which an excess of grape sugar is found in the urine due to a deficiency of the internal secretion of the

---

*The standard specifies: "double dewclaws behind and single dewclaws in front."

pancreas. When a synthetic preparation is made from the islet cells of the pancreas and is injected in the correct quantities into the body, this excess sugar disappears from the urine. Sometimes diabetes leads also to a cataract, which affects the eyesight, and the dog becomes very sluggish. In my opinion, it is kinder to put a dog to sleep if he develops diabetes, as continually repeated injections are the only treatment, and to give him these is not very kind to the animal.

Diarrhea. *If my dog has diarrhea, how can I tell whether he is infected with some disease or whether the cause is purely dietetic?*

This is fairly simple. If the dog doesn't appear ill, has no temperature, and responds quickly to simple remedies and a change of diet, you can be fairly sure that diet, or a slight chill, is the cause. But this looseness of the bowels is an early symptom of so many diseases that if it persists more than one day, you would be very wise to seek expert advice.

Many dogs suffer an intolerance to fat and if their diet happens to contain too much, they promptly get diarrhea. They pass mucus and sometimes blood, and the owner is terrified, but again the response to medication is usually prompt. I am going to let a veterinarian tell you a little more about this subject, as I think it most important.

A veterinarian writes:

> Diarrhea usually results from some irritation in the bowel during the course of an infectious disease or in cases of poisoning. It may commonly occur without other symptoms and may be the result of mild food-poisoning. Where vomiting occurs, it is as well to withhold food for at least 24 hours, and only give water in regulated quantity, preferably with glucose. Again, with diarrhea it is well to withhold food; glucose is useful, and arrowroot and raw eggs will often help. It is impossible to suggest any other than first-aid treatment before the cause of the condition is established.

Dietetics. *I should like to know a little more about the nutrition of dogs. Can you tell me the basic principles?*

The nutritional needs of a dog come under two headings, which can best be called the maintenance ration and the production ration. The former represents a bare minimum of feeding, which may be quite enough for the old dog lying in the chimney corner all day; the latter is for active dogs, or very active dogs like racing greyhounds or working hounds, who need a good deal of extra food to keep them going.

Before we can examine different methods of feeding dogs, we must know a little about the constituents of foods. Food is made up of fats, carbohydrates, and proteins, not forgetting water, salts, and minerals. Vitamins are present in fresh food but can be destroyed by cooking in some cases. When dogs were still wild animals, they chose the food they required in the natural state, and were thus always certain to get what the body required. But nowadays dogs have to rely on the bounty of their owners and would receive punishment for helping themselves from the fowl yard when they felt they wanted a chicken. Therefore owners must provide food that is certain to contain all that the dog needs for perfect health. Animals can live for a considerable time without water but suffer in health as a result of lack of water or water given only spasmodically. Therefore the first rule is to see that there is always a plentiful supply of clean water available day and night for your dog. Without water the dog cannot digest food properly. Carbohydrates are chiefly needed for the production of energy; therefore some kind of biscuits or bread is essential in every dog's diet. Although I have known dogs to keep healthy on a diet of meat alone, how long this would last, I don't know.

Fat provides heat for keeping the dog warm, as well as energy, but excessive fat is bad for the dog and tends to give it a bad heart and other troubles.

A certain amount of fiber is necessary and helps the

passage of waste products in the intestine, though dogs do need less fiber than other domestic animals. Therefore, never mash the dog's food too much, which would produce a doughy mass in the intestine and cause trouble. Some hard food is essential for health.

Protein foods like meat and fish are used to build up muscle. If given in excess, the strain on the kidneys becomes too much and may cause illness. If too much protein is being decomposed in the intestines, it may cause diarrhea. Thus it will be seen that in every case feeding must be balanced for the good health of the dog. Dogs require concentrated food; they are not like cows, who have four stomachs and can regurgitate and chew again what they have eaten. A dog has only one stomach, which must not be abused. Half their diet should be of meat, with occasional changes to fish.

When puppies are being reared, remember that bitches' milk is far richer in fats and casein than cows' milk, and more closely resembles the milk of goats (which many breeders keep for this reason). Cows' milk can be made more like bitches' milk by gently simmering it and getting rid of some of the water.

Normally dogs need only two meals a day, at midday and at night. The biggest meal should always be at night when the dog has time to sleep and digest its food. Hounds are seldom fed daily. They get enormous meals three times a week and seem to keep extremely fit on this diet. It would not suit the ordinary dog-owner to feed his dog in this way, although it is quite a well-known custom to starve a dog one day a week. This I have never done, nor would I like to start it. I think regular mealtimes most important in the life of a healthy dog. The saliva begins to flow at the usual time for a meal, and the digestive juices, if not employed, may cause digestive upsets. If a dog doesn't get his expected meal, you are letting him down, and his faith in you cannot be as strong as it should be. I never let a dog down in any way if I can help it.

Some people feed puppies like human babies, and give them foods like farina, not to mention orange juice and apples. This suits the puppies very well but is not a necessity. Good raw meat, milk, wholemeal bread or biscuits, vitamins, and an occasional egg, and your dog will get everything he needs.

Dietetics—Minerals. *Can you give me any information as to the necessity of providing minerals in dogs' food? How do I give these ingredients?*

Minerals are absolutely essential for the well-being of the dog. They are required for bone formation in the growing animal and for the healthy state of the blood and tissues. Normally a well-balanced diet will contain enough minerals for all the dog's needs, but if the dog doesn't receive enough minerals from his food, the body draws on the bones and tissues. Lack of minerals causes rickets and eczema and, coupled with lack of vitamins A and D, slows recovery after a feverish illness. Some people even hold mineral deficiency responsible for cases of hysteria.

Remember that puppies draw their mineral needs from their dam, so it is especially necessary to provide calcium and phosphorus for the use of the dam's body. Calcium is present in milk and bones or can be given by mouth in pill form or by injection.

Eclampsia in a bitch, a disease that often occurs some days after whelping, is caused by lack of calcium. This is a very dangerous trouble and can cause death if the lack of calcium is not made good by injection. The animal becomes highly excitable and may collapse; veterinary aid must be sought quickly.

Mineral deficiency is suspect in the following cases: if the legs of growing puppies are not straight and bulge at the joints; if their coats are not shiny, and if they are always scratching though they have no infestation by insects.

There are a vast number of products on the market that provide minerals and vitamins and everything else necessary for the dog's health, and nowadays there is ample knowledge of the uses of minerals in the nutrition of the dog. Some people follow the "natural method" of feeding, which includes the sprinkling of seaweed powder on the dog's food. You can find out all you wish on this subject from Organic Herbal Products Ltd., of Bridgwater, Somerset, England. The manufacturers of dog biscuits and prepared dogfoods will send you literature about their products. But for the ordinary dog-owner I suggest plenty of raw meat, milk, an occasional egg, and bones (big marrow bones, not small ones that can splinter). This diet, coupled with wholemeal bread or dog biscuits should keep your dog in perfect health.

Docking. *I am going to breed my Spaniel bitch for the first time. I know the puppies' tails must be docked. Is this done at home? If so, how?*

Even in these enlightened days, breeders are still permitted to mutilate their dogs by docking their tails. This process spoils much of their beauty and makes them objects of fashion; it robs them of their natural balance when running and turning quickly and, in the case of some breeds like Corgis, makes it almost impossible for the dog to show his pleasure by wagging his tail. A vast number of dogs still suffer this indignity, and the length of tail left depends on the breed of dog being docked.

Your letter sounds as if you were a complete amateur, and I don't think any amateur should carry out any operation, however easy, on any animal. If you want your dogs to conform to the standards laid down for the breed, docking must be done and, in my opinion, the best person to do the job is an experienced breeder of the type or breed of dog concerned. From the point of view of the show ring, you can entirely spoil the look of a dog by bad docking, that is leaving the tail too long or cutting it too short. Poodles, for instance, have their tails left fairly long; Boxers, very short.

Some states have laws forbidding docking by anyone other than a veterinarian. If your state has no such law, and if you have studied the requirements of your breed and are not squeamish, you can carry out this minor operation yourself at home. You should have someone assist you by holding the puppies one by one. You need a firm surface on which to lay the tail to be docked and a very sharp, single-edged razor blade. You also need cotton and tincture of benzoin compound, which you apply immediately to act as an antiseptic and to stop the bleeding. The mother will do the rest by licking the wound.

The tail must be severed between the joints of the tail, never through the bone, and an experienced person can plainly feel where this occurs. The cut must be quick, straight, and firmly done to inflict the minimum of pain. Docking should be done at about ten days old, when they do not feel much, and before their eyes are open. I think the poor mother suffers more than the puppies as she frantically licks her bleeding litter. If the tail of an adult dog has to be docked, only a vet should carry this out under an anesthetic.

Ears. *My dog is perpetually shaking and scratching his ears. What should I do?*

The causes of ear trouble are numerous. It may for instance be due to infestation by mange parasites that infest the hair of the outer ear. If this is the case, wash the outer ear with a pesticidal soap or lotion or, in difficult cases, use benzyl benzoate. This has side effects sometimes and should only be used under veterinary supervision. These mange parasites cause scabies in human beings; having once myself been infected with this horrible complaint, I strongly advise owners of dogs afflicted with mange parasites to wear rubber gloves and get expert treatment quickly.

Many people poke their dogs' ears with cotton on matchsticks in the mistaken idea that the inner ear must be cleaned regularly. This is wrong. It is far safer to inject a little warm oil or some aureomycin eardrops into the ear. Then the wax will be lubricated and will come out when the ear is shaken by the dog. The outer ear should always be kept clean from the brown discharge that denotes ear trouble, but usually an infective, not a parasitic one. Aureomycin or other antibiotic eardrops soon clear this up. As soon as the dog holds its head on one side, or shakes it, or scratches it, get expert advice.

Never allow water or soap to enter the inner ear; plug the ear with cotton before treating the outer flap. In breeds like Spaniels, the hair sometimes gets matted and it must then be cut off, or a weeping eczema starts. Calamine lotion and eardrops usually clear up this trouble, once air has been allowed to enter the ear. There is no disease called "canker"; this is only a name that covers a multitude of troubles, coined for lay use. Find out the specific cause, and treat accordingly.

Euthanasia. *I am simply dreading the day when I must say farewell to my dog, as she is now twelve years old and very infirm. I feel she will suffer terribly if I take her to the vet and abandon her to her fate, but what can I do?*

Ask your vet to give you some Nembutal or similar sleeping tablets, and give them to her in her meat. She will fall naturally to sleep in her own home, and the vet can then be called to inject her with a fatal dose. She will know nothing and feel nothing. You owe this to a faithful friend, so do not shirk your duty, however terrible for you.

Exercising. *I am not at all fit. I would love to own a dog but fear that the amount of exercise I can give it is not very* *much. Would I be unkind if I could not give it long walks?*

A lot of nonsense is talked about exercising dogs. Most people are exercising themselves more than the dog when they stroll round the town window-shopping, or walk twice around the block at night.

If you cannot give your dog walks, you can let it out to amuse itself in the garden if you have one and if the weather is fine. Or the dog could be tethered by a chain to a long wire, and run up and down on that; perhaps some kind friend would help by taking the dog walking, or you might hire a responsible child to take the dog out. I think few people who really love dogs and need their companionship should be denied the pleasure of walking their dogs.

A lot of people, many of them elderly folk who should be looking after their own health, make martyrs of them-selves exercising dogs in all weathers. Do the best you can for your pet, and he will not hold it against you that he has missed the smells of the countryside. Dogs soon accustom themselves to a certain routine when they know no other. Dogs run about the house quite happily when young; when old they do not need much exercise.

In view of your infirmity, I do think that you should be most careful in the type of dog you choose. I think you should buy a tiny toy dog and would suggest an older dog rather than a puppy. If possible, choose one that might be likely to want to chase a ball for exercise. Yorkshire terriers are very sporting and will retrieve a ball for as long as you like to throw one. Neither Pomeranians nor Papillons need much exercise.

While I am on this subject of exercise, I would stress to all owners that some dogs need masses of exercise to keep them happy and free from annoying habits and vices. Some dogs need to follow a master or mistress on foot or on horseback for miles each day (or even follow a car if properly trained to stay on the side of the road). Some dogs are never still, they are always begging to be taken out.

These are tiresome dogs to own if you are a busy person. Yet there is no particular breed of which one can say firmly that they need tons of exercise. I have known Boxers who were never still, and I know Boxers who can hardly be dragged out for a walk. It is all according to the individual makeup of particular dogs. It also depends on the initial training when the dog first comes into your home. You may at first be so thrilled with owning a dog that you take it out for long walks daily. The dog loves this and begins to know the routine. As the owner's new enthusiasm wears thin, the dog gets less and less exercise, and thereby hangs a tale: for this is what makes a dog tear things up and become a problem to handle. They are creatures of routine, so start as you really mean to go on, and don't get carried away in the beginning by enthusiasm you cannot hope to maintain.

Exercise has two sides to it. There is the essential amount of movement necessary to keep the dog in good health, and the extra exercise that gives the dog, and possibly the owner, pleasure but that is not a necessity. The first *must* be given, the second need not. A dog picks up its owner's moods and, in some cases, never asks for a walk if it thinks its owner is too worried or busy to go out—yet the slightest sign of a changed mood on the owner's part and the dog is waiting and ready to have fun. That is the joy of owning an intelligent dog.

I know I have strayed beyond the scope of my correspondent's question. Only she can really know whether life for her dog would be a happy one; but if there were not far more to a dog's happiness than exercise, my own dogs might be unhappy, busy person that I am.

Eyelids. *My four-year-old Collie has an inverted eyelid, which makes the eye very sore; a friend of mine has a Setter with inflamed eyelids, which show no lasting improvement after being bathed with eye lotion. What causes these conditions, and how can they be cured?*

Inverted eyelids are fairly easy to deal with. I don't think there is agreement as to what causes them; some say it is hereditary, others that it is caused by inflammation of the conjunctiva, or lining of the lids. The cure is to take away by surgery an elliptical piece of skin from the outer surface of the eyelid and stitch the edges together again, which causes the lashes to turn outward once more. The dog suffers very little discomfort. The opposite sort of thing sometimes happens in dogs—that is, the turning outward of the conjunctiva or lining of the eyelid—and then the operation is to remove part of the conjunctiva from the inside of the lid. This condition is normal in dogs like Bloodhounds and St. Bernards but can look very nasty in other dogs.

While we are on the subject of eyes, I should mention that dogs sometimes get warts on their eyelids. These warts spread at an alarming rate and, in my opinion, should have expert veterinary advice and treatment immediately they are noticed, or blindness may ensue.

Inflammation of the eyelids is termed blepharitis; it can be extremely dangerous and can cause blindness although, in these days of cortisone and other drugs, better treatment can be hoped for. It is not a disease that should be treated at home, and I strongly advise you to consult your vet without delay. It may be a simple condition caused by dust or a seed in the eye, or it may not. If the dog has blepharitis, he will probably have an intolerance to light, so keep him in a darkened room until the vet comes.

Fawning. *When visitors come to the house, my dog is a perfect pest; she fawns and slobbers all over them and quite ruins their pleasure. What can I do?*

No dog can be a nuisance if trained to lie down when told. If your dog disobeys this order or gets up again too soon, she must be taught that the next few seconds are going to be really unpleasant for her. Reading between the lines of your query, I think you may be rather easygoing and let the dog play you up—I suggest therefore a visit to your nearest training school. There you will be shown how to make your dog lie down and stay down: a matter of making her understand that when you say "down," you mean it, of scolding and being really firm if she disobeys, and of patiently repeating this process until she does as you say. Your dog should also benefit from contact with a professional trainer, who will not so easily tolerate disobedience.

Feeding Puppies. *I have bought a new puppy for my daughter. Everyone tells me something different about how I should feed it. What are the main points to bear in mind?*

There are few hard and fast rules about feeding dogs. Like babies, puppies vary enormously in what they like and what is good for them, and their appetites vary even within the same litter.

When the puppy first comes into your home at about eight to ten weeks or even earlier, it must be fed four or five times a day according to its appetite. Small meals, easily digested, should be the rule. The diet should include raw ground beef, milk, brown bread or puppy meal, and a plentiful supply of clean water. Additional vitamins should be added to the diet to ensure freedom from rickets; cod-liver oil or vitamins A, D, and B, in pill or liquid form, are important for health and growth.

It is impossible to lay down exact amounts for each puppy, but in the main they should have two meat meals a day and two milk meals. Gradually reduce this number to two a day so that at about six to eight months the puppy has only one or two meals a day. To ensure sleep at night, give the biggest meal last.

Nowadays there are so many prepared dogfoods available, each with full instructions enclosed, that no one, however lacking in knowledge, need feed their dog wrongly.

However, what will make one puppy thrive will upset another. I have often found that it is necessary to change a puppy's brand of food, not because there is anything wrong with that brand but because it just doesn't suit that particular animal.

Vegetables are not, as many people believe, a necessity. Some puppies love them, and they certainly do no harm, but they do not form part of a dog's natural diet. Bones are not really good for dogs—they not only cause constipation but can so easily splinter and lead to internal injury—but puppies do like a big shinbone to grind their teeth on. Meat for puppies should of course be ground, and the occasional addition of such things as egg or liver to the diet can do nothing but good.

Chocolates, sweets, and highly seasoned foods are good for neither puppies nor fully grown dogs, and begging for scraps from the humans' table must be firmly discouraged. Let the puppies be fed at their own mealtimes only.

Fighting. *I shall be buying a dog shortly. I have always liked the look of a Kerry Blue, but friends tell me they are born fighters. Are there special breeds that fight more than others? If there are, and if I come to own such a dog, how can I teach it not to be aggressive? If it gets involved in a fight, how can I extricate it?*

I agree with your friends that you are choosing a breed of dog that is well known for its fighting tendencies. In the past most of the Terrier breeds have been used for sport of some kind or other, and breeds like Bull Terriers, Irish Terriers, Staffordshire Terriers, Wirehaired Terriers, and some strains of Boxers do love to have a go at other dogs. There are of course good and bad temperaments in every breed, and I believe that with proper training you can make practically any dog behave. If you get an incurable fighter, castration helps enormously, but the most important thing is to correct your dog from an early age by terrific jerks on the choke chain and the command "Leave" if he shows any signs of being pugnacious. Take him to a training school to mix with other dogs, and let him, when young, play with other dogs as much as possible. In towns, take him on a loose lead, never shortening it as you meet other dogs but just giving an almighty jerk instead. That is all you should have to do to train your dog. If you think he is going to fight, he undoubtedly will pick up your thoughts, and a fight might ensue. Therefore, if you are of a nervous disposition, do not buy a breed you suspect of being fighters. Actually I have known fighters in practically every breed, but of course the bigger the dog, the more difficult it will be to control. If, however, you like these game breeds of dogs and are not frightened of having to separate them should they get into a fight, by all means have one. They are great fun to own and very affectionate and faithful.

In case of a dog fight involving one of the bull breeds like Bulldogs, Boxers, or Bullmastiffs, you will find them difficult to separate owing to their teeth placement and the shape of their jaws. Choking them with their choke chains or lifting them by the loose skin between the ears on the forehead are the two best methods, but you will need help to keep the fighters apart when you have separated them. It is far better to train your dog not to fight. I have had my own bitch attacked by wandering dogs in the street, and even though she didn't answer back, it gave me a nasty fright. I really think the best thing to do, if you live in a neighborhood of belligerent dogs, is to carry a walking stick, train your own dog to "downstay," and, on the approach of another dog that looks like fighting, crack it a hard one before it can reach your dog. Until owners are forced by law to keep their dogs under control, we shall always suffer from the attention of these menaces, and we who train our dogs properly feel most bitter about them.

Filmwork. *I think my dog is awfully clever, and I should love him to act in films. What do I have to make him do to be useful for this work, and how should I set about making him an actor?*

Whereas in England people seeking TV and film careers for their animals apply directly to the networks and studios, in the United States they work through animal talent agencies. Most of these agencies are in New York or on the West Coast. Dog-owners can write for an application, and when they return it, they should include photographs of the dog—snapshots will do, as long as they are good and clear; at least one photograph should be in color. If the agency is interested in your dog, they will contact you for an interview.

Agencies usually accept only dogs between one and five years of age. Young puppies are too bumptious, as well as delicate, and older dogs might suffer cruelly from fatigue and from the hot lights, which have been known to cause heat prostration in animals.

All-black dogs do not show up well on film; neither do all-white ones. Brown (not too dark), tan, or beige dogs photograph best, and particolored dogs with clear markings.

Breed matters, too. Dogs with unfriendly associations and images—Bloodhounds, Dobermans, German Shepherds —are not in much demand.

Discipline and temperament, of course, are what count most. Film dogs must be of patient disposition and not given to wilting easily. They must be very well trained, as the cost of wasting film on badly trained dogs is enormous. Your dog must obey commands or signals to stay anywhere, to come on a whistle, call or signal from anywhere even with you out of sight. He must sit on command, lie down, play dead, beg, carry objects, jump up on things, bark on command, go with anyone, eat food or refuse food as told. With these achievements he can be most useful. With further achievements like attacking without biting, he can go a very long way.

The hours are long usually, and are normally taken up by sitting about and doing nothing. There is little glamour in filmwork, yet the thrill of seeing your own dog on the screen makes up for all the boredom while shooting.

Directors and scriptwriters often ask you to make your dog do things dogs never do, so when you see the script, say outright what the dog can or cannot do, or the company will be misled. Expect little or no praise from anyone even though you may think your dog was perfectly wonderful. To the powers that be, your dog is just another piece of property.

Your dog will get a lot of petting from studio hands and actors, which tires him out and makes him almost unfit for work. You must tactfully ask them to leave him in peace. Have plenty of water handy at all times as the lights make a dog thirsty. Under no circumstances feed your dog if he is to work; that makes a dog want to sleep. Take him for frequent airings outdoors or he will go to sleep. Be sure the film company insures him; nails are constantly left on studio floors, scenery falls down, and people are forever moving things about.

Take a book to read and keep out of everyone's way; above all, don't address the director—if you want to know anything, ask the production manager. The director may be thinking, and if you interrupt those vital thoughts, you will not be popular.

Filmwork is not an easy profession to gate-crash. The pay sounds good, but the work one gets in twelve months is not a lot. If you are used, however, it does prove that you know how to train a dog.

First Aid and Home Treatment of Injuries. *Can you tell me something about first aid for dogs and the home treatment of canine injuries?*

I think every household with a dog in it should have a first-aid box, clearly labeled with the contents, and possibly a list of what to do in an emergency. It is extraordinary how many people panic when somthing has happened to their dog.

I will deal first with cuts. These can be little more than scratches, or they can be deep cuts, which need expert attention. The way to tell whether a severe cut has severed an artery or not is by watching how the blood comes. If it comes in a pumping fashion in time with the pulse, there is severance of the artery, and bleeding must be stopped at all costs or you may lose your dog. In this case the best method to stop the bleeding is to apply a tourniquet above the wound. Wrap a clean handkerchief around the limb, if the injury is in a leg or paw, putting a pencil into the handkerchief, and twisting until the bleeding stops. The pressure should be applied above the wound and on the side of the injury nearest the heart. It is important not to have the tourniquet too tight so that it harms the limb, but just tight enough to stop the bleeding. It should be loosened every ten minutes or so to see if the bleeding is arrested. If the bleeding comes from a vein, in which case the flow of blood will be regular and the color not as bright, the tourniquet should be applied below the injury. If this is not possible, apply pressure over a pad directly on the wound.

The dog should have veterinary aid as soon as possible, and any deep or very ragged wound is best stitched by a vet. It is not often that such bad injuries occur among dogs except when they are injured on the road or cut by wire or glass. But dogs do often receive minor scratches and cuts; if these are washed with 10% volume hydrogen peroxide or other antiseptic solution and kept clean afterward, they heal very rapidly.

Normally wounds heal by what we term "granulating inward." Granulations are small masses of cells containing loops of freshly formed blood vessels that form on the healing surface of the wound and, in multiplying, close in the wound until the whole surface is healed over. Occasionally this process gets out of hand and excessive granulation takes place; this is known as "proud flesh." The wound with proud flesh will not heal, and that part above the surface of the wound must be burned back with a silver nitrate stick, after which normal healing will occur. Dogs so often keep wounds open by licking them that where the wound can have a stitch, it has more likelihood of healing quickly.

I loathe iodine for first aid. It can be extremely dangerous owing to its tendency to seal the wound and shut the germs in. Also some dogs are sensitive to iodine and the reaction is worse than the wound. I prefer to use an antibiotic solution or ointment as an antiseptic.

A bruise is a contusion in which the skin is not broken. The bleeding occurs under the skin, hence the discoloration of the tissues. Bruises need cold-water bandages or the hose gently running over them. I have found homeopathic tincture of calendula makes an excellent cold compress diluted with water and applied on a pad to the bruise. I used it extensively in Argentina for humans and animals when they got hurt. It can be bought from any druggist who stocks homeopathic remedies.

Occasionally dogs get grass seeds in their eyes and are in terrible pain. The first-aid treatment is castor oil in the eye as quickly as possible; then take the dog to the vet. He will examine the eye for serious damage by staining the eye with fluorescence, which remains in the scratch but washes off the normal uninjured surface. Should there be a scratch on the cornea, cortisone drops are usually instilled into the eye, and healing takes place. It is essential to stop the dog from rubbing the injured eye.

Sometimes grass seeds enter the ear and cause of lot of trouble. Once again, beyond putting a little warm oil into the ear, you can do nothing; it is an expert's job, because with an auriscope, which looks rather like a flashlight, the vet can look right into the ear and remove the offending grass seed.

Burns and scalds have been known to occur when the household dog has bumped into the busy housewife and caused her to spill boiling water over it. The first-aid treatment is to cut off the hair and apply moist bicarbonate of soda to the affected part. If it is a third-degree burn with a blister, don't break the blister. Cover it up with bicarbonate of soda, and place a damp clean rag over it. Get qualified aid quickly. In all cases of severe injury the dog is probably suffering from shock and should be kept warm by a fire or with a blanket. If it will drink some warm milk, that helps to combat shock.

If you suspect that a dog has a fracture, don't move him. Apply a splint and bandage lightly. Nowadays dogs get X-rayed like human beings and have every chance of a complete recovery.

Choking is sometimes met with in dogs and is very frightening for the owner. If a piece of bone is choking the dog, you should try to dislodge it by crooking your little finger and making an effort to bring the offending piece of bone back. Occasionally the bone can be brought back by holding the dog up by its tail and giving it a shake. In my opinion, bones, unless they are unbroken shinbones, should never be given to dogs.

Foster Mothers and Hand-Rearing. *My tiny toy Poodle bitch is due to have puppies at any time. People tell me I should have a foster mother ready to take over some of the puppies as these tiny Poodles do not rear many puppies alone. What is your advice?*

I wonder what makes you think the bitch is going to have so many puppies that she will not be able to feed them? In the vast majority of cases, nature provides the mother with adequate milk to feed the number she produces. There are of course cases where the milk supply of the dam is inadequate and the foster mother must be quickly found, or hand-rearing resorted to, which is a terrible job. Check the dog magazines for advertisements of foster mothers in your area. I feel sure you would be happier if you contacted these people and made sure that they had a foster mother available at about the time you wanted one. I am assuming that you do not know any dog breeder near you who might have puppies arriving at about the same time and who might in an emergency be willing for her bitch to suckle one or two of your puppies. Your vet may know where a foster mother can be obtained. Sometimes a cat with newly born kittens will suckle a puppy with great affection. Local newspapers and radio stations are often willing to send out pleas for foster mothers. In any case, if you hire a foster mother, she will arrive with her own puppies as well and must be returned to her owner when the puppies are weaned.

If the puppies are reared by hand, a bottle and nipples can be bought at the druggist or at pet shops for this purpose. The bottles and nipples must be kept scrupulously clean, and the puppies must be fed every two hours day and night to begin with. A breeder gave me the following recipe for making cows' milk equal to bitches' milk:

Mix five ounces of cold water with three level tablespoonfuls of a concentrate like Similac; then add ¾ pint of cold milk. Boil gently for two or three minutes and let it get cold. Keep it in the refrigerator and warm to body temperature (100° F.) before feeding the puppies. Before using it, add three tablespoonfuls of fresh cream, as bitches' milk is nearly four times as rich in fat as cows' milk.

Friendliness, Indiscriminate. *My dog loves everyone; she would as soon go away with a burglar as bite one. I have asked people in the street not to pet her, but her limpid eyes and long Cocker's ears make her a target for general affection. How can I teach her to ignore strangers?*

Quite honestly, I don't think you can, for if you got all your friends to scold her or smack her as she approached them, she would simply become shy and nervous, horrible traits in any dog. You do not mention her age. Youngsters are nearly all friendly, so if she is twelve months or under, I shouldn't worry. But if she is nearer two years old, I should start a fixed course of training and enter her for obedience tests at shows. This would make her far more attentive to you, and she would live for your commands and praise. This is what most dogs lack, and therefore they seek other people's love as well as that of their owners. Keep her with you all the time; don't turn her out in the garden to play but take her for walks. You yourself must be her "be all and end all." Ask a few friends to send her back to you if she approaches them in too friendly a manner.

Glands. *What are glands and their functions? I am always hearing of somebody's dog having swollen glands.*

I think the way the dictionary answers this vast question is extremely neat. It simply says: "A gland is a structure for secreting substances to be used in or eliminated from the body."

The layman probably doesn't realize what a vast number of different glands there are in the body. The ones dog-owners come in contact with most are the parotid gland situated below and behind the ear, the submaxillary gland placed in the angle of the lower jaw, and the sublingual gland beneath the tongue, because all are busy making saliva, and few owners haven't seen their dogs dribbling at the sight of food.

In fact all the major organs in the body like the liver, kidneys, ovaries, and pancreas are glands secreting products vital for the smooth running of bodily functions. The thyroid gland is most important; so are the adrenal glands, which, in conjunction with the pituitary gland, govern the hormone activities of the body. Sex functions are largely dependent on these glands. Lymph glands are important because they filter off bacteria traveling away from an infected area and thus stop the spread of the infection. In doing so, they themselves become swollen; for example, the glands in the neck swell when a dog has a sore throat or tonsillitis and are therefore a helpful sign of this condition, which you might otherwise not notice. In castration the sex glands of the male dog are removed.

The anal glands placed at the side of the anus can cause a lot of trouble in dogs. These are considered to be scent glands and secrete a horrid musky-smelling liquid. They often get overfull, and the dog drags its backside along the floor in an effort to relieve them. The result is constipation if the glands are not relieved by having the fluid squeezed out, which a vet will do. Occasionally they need surgical removal.

Grass-Eating. *My dog eats grass. Does it lack vegetables, or vitamins? If not, why does it do it?*

This grass-eating is purely and simply the dog's method of making itself sick and relieving some indisposition of the digestion. Bilious dogs do it to get rid of the excessive bile built up in the stomach and, after being sick, will very often feel quite all right and be ready for a meal.

I have heard it said that dogs left to wander in the countryside eat all sorts of greenstuffs, which is taken to mean that they lack vegetables in their diet. I have never had this happen with my own dogs or other people's dogs I have boarded, so I am inclined to think that a dog properly fed does not indulge in this habit.

Grooming. *I am a very busy dog-owner and seldom seem to have time for grooming my Dobermann Pinscher. Is grooming really necessary? His coat always seems to look so clean and shiny in spite of the fact that I seldom give him much attention.*

You are lucky in owning a short-coated dog. Grooming aids circulation and the casting of the old coat; it helps the skin to breathe by friction and is excellent for promoting health in dogs. I think a good bath once a month with a good dog soap also does this for a dog, but if your dog seems perfectly healthy-coated and clean, the answer must be, "Why worry?"

Most dogs need some grooming, however perfunctory. Some dogs need a tremendous amount of care of the coat, and my answer must be that if you want a dog in tiptop condition, groom him even if it is only once a week. A glove brush is the most suitable for short-coated dogs; a wire brush and comb are best for long-haired dogs. Some people carry out their own stripping; a stripping comb with one sharp edge specially made for the job can be used. Some dogs are far more sensitive than others. When you groom your dog, be careful not to be rough or you will make him bad-tempered; I have a lot of pupils in my training schools who come because they bite while they are being groomed. Groom firmly but gently—remember how it hurts you to have your hair pulled! On the other hand, you must be firm about carrying out grooming, irrespective of the dog's wishes; once he learns that you stop grooming him when he bites, the seed is well and truly sown.

There are two types of hair in most dogs' coats, the overlength hair, which is the coarse long hair, and the undercoat, which is the soft hair underneath. In dogs like German Shepherds this makes the coat completely waterproof. In trimming a dog, it is the long overlength hairs that should be plucked out, leaving the softer undercoat intact. That is why just clipping instead of plucking the coat out is not so good for the dog as correct stripping, which gets rid of the loose old hair.

Terriers need trimming three or four times a year, and unless you are very good at it, I think it is better to take them to a professional stripper. A terrier badly done looks awful, and the same applies to Poodles and Cockers. The cost, we know, adds up, but if money is very tight, I do not imagine you would buy a dog that needed a lot of grooming. The hair from long-coated dogs is useful for weaving and can be saved in clean bags and sold.

Hard Pad. *How can I protect my dog from getting distemper or hard pad?*

Most dog-owners in the past lived in fear and terror that their beloved dogs might catch distemper or hard pad and die. Today the risk is not nearly so great; inoculations give reasonably good protection, and most owners feel fairly safe taking their dogs everywhere with them. But it is possible to have a modified attack of either of these diseases, so if the dog is off color, take his temperature and seek veterinary advice. No form of protection is absolutely safe. The dog should be inoculated at about three to four months and kept away from other dogs for another month until a reasonable immunity has been set up; some owners also like to give their dogs a boosting dose if they are going to a big show some years after the original vaccination.

As with all diseases, there is much less risk of the dog's getting ill if sensible precautions are taken about drying him when he gets wet, not letting him lie in cold, drafty places, keeping him away from other dogs that have had anything wrong with them, and noticing the state of his bowel movements. If the dog shows any signs of a sore throat or of going off his food, get expert advice. Prevention is always easier than cure. Should the dog get shivery, have diarrhea, and be constantly sick, take his temperature; if that is over 101.5° F., keep him warm and call your vet. It may be only a chill, but play safe.

Quite a number of people think it very wrong to inoculate dogs to protect them. They maintain that with correct feeding methods and healthy surroundings dogs build up a natural immunity and escape all these diseases. I respect their views but do not agree with them. I should never forgive myself if my beloved dog died from hard pad because I had more faith in nature than in science. I once saw a young man die from a perforated appendix because his mother did not believe in doctors. I have never got over it. Hundreds of people don't get perforated appendixes, and hundreds of dogs would never get hard pad or distemper even if they were not inoculated. I do agree that sensible feeding methods and healthy living conditions make the dog doubly safe. But as with modern inoculation against polio, I think we can protect our children and our dogs by profiting from knowledge gained through scientific methods, so I have asked our vet to elaborate a little on this subject. He writes:

Canine distemper has been known for very many years to be one of the most important infectious diseases of dogs. It has also been known for some time that it is caused by a virus, that is to say, an extremely small organism which cannot be seen even in the ordinary microscope. More recently hard pad has been described as a separate disease, also caused by a virus, and being in many ways similar to distemper. Nowadays it is largely thought that there is a third type of distemper-like disease. It is not certain whether there are three entirely different viruses or whether one virus has the ability to change its characteristics. The exact diagnosis of the three types of disease is very difficult. The effect of the virus is to depress the animal, to cause a rise in temperature and to lower the resistance so that other germs can gain entry. The original viruses very frequently attack the nervous system. The early signs of the disease are those of depression, loss of appetite, and high temperature. Frequently cough, pneumonia, vomiting and diarrhea develop during the course of the disease and, if the central nervous system has suffered damage by the virus, then fits, convulsions and the so-called chorea, or paralysis, may develop. The incubation period may vary from a few days to as much as three weeks and the course of the disease may be several weeks.

In the hard pad type the pads and nose may harden up in the later stages of the disease but this is not a consistent symptom.

Treatment should always be under professional direction but good nursing is absolutely vital. Fortunately there is a most effective preventative inoculation which gives very good protection against both distemper and hard pad and it can be given any time after about 12 weeks of age.

A serum is also of value in the treatment of early cases.

If nervous symptoms arise the outlook is very grave, and few such cases fully recover.

House-Training. *I have bought a two-year-old dog who is not house-trained. I know how to train a puppy, but this dog doesn't respond to any of the normal encouragement or scolding. He lifts his leg over sofas and other objects. What can I do?*

The remedy is simply to confine the dog in an indoor kennel that is just big enough for him to stand up, turn around, and lie down comfortably, but not big enough to allow him the freedom to lift his leg. Take him out if possible for a nice walk every two hours and then put him back in his kennel. This should house-train a dog in roughly forty-eight hours. If it does not, the dog is probably over-sexed; have him castrated.

Hysteria. *What is the cause of hysteria? My eight-month-old puppy suddenly goes mad and doesn't even seem to know me; he shrieks the place down and the neighbors think I am ill-treating him.*

It is difficult to say whether the hysteria apparent in your dog is due to worms, teething troubles, or heredity. The most common cause of hysteria in dogs, apart from those causes I have just mentioned, is the use of white bread or the wrong type of biscuits. White bread contains a bleaching agent called agene, which seems to set up an alimentary toxemia in dogs, ultimately causing hysteria.

The first-aid treatment for hysteria is to see that the dog doesn't hurt himself. Then make sure he is free from worms, and has his diet changed. While he is actually having a fit, the dog should be placed in a cool, dark place, as he will not be able to stand light. Get your vet to prescribe a sedative; feed the dog on wholemeal bread or biscuits, and also give him a course of vitamin B complex, available in tablet form. There are many types of manufactured dog biscuits and meals that are perfectly adequate in providing a suitable diet; get in touch with the manufacturers and ask them to recommend the special variety best suited for dogs suffering from hysteria.

Inoculations. *I have a new puppy and naturally want to do everything I can to make him a healthy and happy dog. I am worried over inoculating him against disease. Some people tell me he is likely to get ill if I have him inoculated with the germs, even though I know they are supposed to prevent the diseases. What do you advise?*

There are always people ready to tell you of the awful things that happen in life, whatever you do. The risk of anything happening to your puppy after being inoculated is so small that I personally would never worry about it. Some inoculations have dead germs in them, some have modified live ones that have been rendered just strong enough to do their job, which is to give the animal enough of them to encourage the body to make enough antibodies to set up a future resistance to that disease. In humans, smallpox vaccination is one of this type, which is why babies get the reactions they do; yet few sensible mothers would deny their babies this safeguard against such a horrible disease as smallpox. You should look at inoculations against hard pad and distemper in the same light. Because millions of dogs are protected by these inoculations, these terrible diseases are slowly being wiped out.

There are, however, one or two things you ought to do

when your dog is inoculated, and the first is to make sure your vet does not give the injection in the shoulder. This has been known to make the dog snappy for the rest of his life when people go to stroke it. Always insist on its being done in the soft part over the tummy in front of the hind leg. The dog, if held, won't even see it being done and, by the time he feels it, the job will be finished.

Take special care that the puppy doesn't get chilled or come too much in contact with other dogs for about a month after inoculation. It takes that time for a reasonable immunity to be built up. Don't take it to shows, but you are unlikely to do this anyway because dogs may not be shown until six months old under Kennel Club rules, and the hard pad and distemper inoculation should take place at three and a half to four months old.

There are one or two other inoculations that I strongly recommend. The first is against leptospiral jaundice and the other against leptospiral nephritis, both killing diseases that few dog-owners seem to have heard about. I have known dogs to die extremely rapidly with the jaundice infection, and, unless the disease is caught early, there is little hope of a cure.

I have had my own dogs given all the inoculations possible for their protection. My Great Dane Juno is a famous film star worth thousands of dollars, and I would not have risked her life for one second had I doubted in any way the safety of having her inoculated. That should be recommendation enough for most dog-owners!

Instinct. *To what extent are dogs guided by instinct? Can one train dogs to forget their natural instincts and just obey without question?*

The relevant meaning of instinct given in a dictionary is as follows: "The natural impulse apparently independent of reason or experience by which animals are guided." To me this sounds very sensible. Take a puppy: every time he is asked to do something he doesn't want to do, or if he fears the approach of a bigger or fiercer dog than himself, he quickly lies on the floor with his legs in the air and tummy exposed to the enemy. This attitude has come down through generations of domesticated dogs; yet it is the remains of an instinct of the wild. For in the wild no young puppy would have been attacked in this position; it is against the laws of nature. This habit is a great hindrance in training, for when a dog does it and you try to put his lead on, he just waves his legs in the air and bites, especially if you try to get hold of his collar. Therefore we must train these dogs to understand that this position will not save them from being made to do what we wish them to do. If they try it with me, I jerk them very quickly into the upright position.

I think dogs are guided a lot by instinct, but a lot more by smell, and I think that smell can vary considerably with individual persons, according to their state of mind. For example, why is it that dogs take instantly to some people and won't go near others, especially when those they don't wish to know want to be friends with them? I think each human being has a friendly or unfriendly smell, which dogs can always detect. Fear, I believe, sends out an unpleasant smell, for dogs sense nervous people yards away.

Why do dogs go and sniff at the base of another dog's tail? It is the old instinct to find out whether that dog belongs to his pack or another by the scent from the anal glands. Why do dogs roll in something dirty, in spite of knowing quite well they will get beaten or bathed for their sin? Because in the old times of wild dogs they wanted to show their enemies they were about, by leaving their own scent on something not carrying it. That is also why they lift their legs where any other dog has lifted his leg; a dog's particular scent indicates to his pack where he has gone.

Certainly one cannot give in to instinct when training a dog to be obedient. A dog must do as he is told without question, providing the thing he is asked to do is fair and reasonable. I do not think jumping through fire is fair or reasonable, and I hate to see animals made to do it as a trick. Animals have an instinctive fear of fire from the old days of forest fires, and to train them to do this trick must, in my opinion, involve a certain amount of cruelty.

Wherever possible we use the dog's natural instincts if they can be guided into the right channels. Take tracking, for example. A dog's natural instinct is to find food by using his nose, and I think most trainers agree that food at the end of the trail is a great incentive when teaching a dog to track; anyway, that is how I train. In my opinion, the more highly bred a dog is, the less instinct it possesses. The stray mongrel reverts to type very often, only coming out to hunt for food at night and snapping at anyone who tries to catch him. That is the ancient instinct to stay free, and I feel that if there were stray bitches about at the same time, that particular dog would soon have a pack living with him. The old instinct of turning around and around and around, making a hole in the ground to sleep in, still persists in the domestic dog today. Most of them turn around two or three times before settling down to sleep, yet they don't make the floor any more comfortable by doing so. The old instinct of bone-burying for future consumption still remains strong in our dogs, although they hardly ever remember where they have buried them, as they are not usually hungry enough. It takes training to make a dog stop digging up the garden to bury his bone, but it can be done.

Intelligence. *One hears extravagant claims about dogs being almost human and "understanding every word." How much do you really think a dog understands, and what are his reasoning powers?*

First of all one must investigate what means a dog has of understanding and reasoning. He has a well-developed brain and an acute sense of hearing. He has first-class eyesight that can see prey move almost imperceptibly in the under-growth, and he has a very acute sense of smell. Added to all these, he has an excellent memory, and a conscience. He has instinct and indisputable psychic powers—how else could a dog know when his owner's car, and his beloved owner, were approaching but still some miles away, or sense his owner's impending departure? All these things and a lot more, no one in their senses disputes, for the evidence is overwhelming. Therefore, when owners say of beloved dogs that they understand every word that is said to them, I think they mean that they understand sounds rather than individual words. The meaning of words is conveyed to a dog by the tone of voice and by the scent from the owner; sweat, for example, has a strong smell, which often conveys fear to a dog. Association of ideas is well known in the dog world, and it is by this method that we train dogs. We teach them what pleases us so that they get praise and love, and what displeases us. They learn to recognize noises of dinner-time, they pick up the owners' thoughts about whether to take the dog for a walk or not, and owners then think it is the word "walk" that the dog understands. Undoubtedly the dog does understand the word but has also understood the thought, and I believe if the owner said "carrots" in the same tone of voice ordinarily used for walks, the dog would get the interpretation.

Recently I was driving down our common and my dog was five hundred yards behind the car sniffing and taking her own time to come on, as I allow on these occasions. Suddenly I thought I might turn up a parallel road and go back. I did or said nothing, I only thought about it, yet my dog stopped expectantly at that turning. She had picked up my thought five hundred yards away without any other indication of what I was going to do. Explain that away if you can.

I believe that by being constantly with the owners, by listening to conversation, and by connecting certain sounds with certain actions, a dog can and does understand about four hundred words, more if he is a well-loved, extremely intelligent dog. Dogs work out for themselves how to avoid scoldings for wrongdoing, and how to get what they want, without the owner meaning to give it to them, by being particularly winning in their ways. They know when to sympathize with the owner by a gentle contact of the muzzle with the owner's hand or knee and by that look of adoration in their eyes. Dogs may not be human, but some are not far off in intelligence.

If you asked dog lovers for stories, you could fill many books with accounts of the clever things dogs do, and obtain proof by the thousand words that dogs understand more than we all realize. Generations of contact with men, aided by their senses of sight, smell, and hearing, have made them truly companions of man.

Interest During Training. *I want to train my Boxer bitch, but she flops around the training class showing no interest at all. I have tried feeding her tidbits, but that only works while the tidbit is offered. Can you give me any hints as to how interest in me and her work can be developed?*

Every person who wants to make a dog thoroughly obedient, and happy as well, has to learn how to gain the dog's interest. I train many hundreds of owners each year, and it depresses me how dull and flat in voice and spirit many of them are. First of all, remember that a dog can't concentrate for a great length of time, so when you are training your bitch, do so only in short spells. Speak in an excited, keen voice; give really hard jerks on the choke chain, not half-hearted ones. Praise with joy in your voice and laughter in your eyes; in fact, try to have that little extra something that makes a dog want your love and appreciation. If you move slowly, give commands in a dull, slow voice, and don't mind terribly whether the dog does the exercise very well or not, you will never have a dog that is interested in her work. Enthusiasm is catching, whether you are dealing with dogs or with human beings. If the dog does wrong, shake her or jerk her hard on the choke chain. After that she will watch your every movement, waiting for the return of your loving mood. She will be thrilled if you praise her when she does what you want.

So few people have the power of making everything in work or play seem fun. I suppose their home lives aren't terribly interesting. Unfortunately dogs mirror their owners, and a dull owner makes a dull, uninterested dog. Cultivate pep and your dog will be enchanted with your every command.

Jaundice. *I have heard that jaundice in dogs is a very dangerous disease. Please tell me how it occurs and what I should do to treat it.*

There are so many different causes of jaundice that it is better first of all to explain what we mean by the term. The name derives from the yellow color of the mucous membranes of the body—those of eye, nose, mouth, etc.—when they are affected by jaundice, which is caused by a deposit of bile pigments in their deep layers. Actually the bile is not able to escape into the small intestine via the bile duct from the liver, as it should in the ordinary way. When it is thus stopped, it is absorbed by the lymphatics and blood vessels and carried back into circulation, and some gets deposited in the tissues, causing the typical yellow coloring. Jaundice may be caused by a blockage of feces due to acute constipation or inflammation of the mucous membrane of the bile ducts themselves. It may be due to worms, distemper, pregnancy, or just old age. The symptoms may be acute or chronic. The ordinary dog-owner probably first notices the clay-colored feces and the bright yellow urine; vomiting is often present and so, sometimes, are fits. The vomit is brown or greenish and very frothy.

In chronic cases the tummy of the dog droops owing to

the dropsical condition of the abdomen, and there is then little hope of recovery. In the acute form the temperature runs extremely high, and immediate veterinary help should be sought. If the disease is caused by obstruction, an operation must be performed; if it is an infective jaundice, antibiotics will be used. Very careful nursing is essential, with the twin objects of keeping the dog warm and of keeping up its strength. Give it whites of egg for this purpose, never the yolks.

Jumping in Obedience Trials. *I am intensely interested in obedience trials and wish to get to the top with my Great Dane, but I see in the premium list for the obedience trials that it is essential for a dog to do a high and broad jump. I feel this might hurt my dog. What do you think?*

I think very high jumps are dangerous for big dogs like Great Danes—their conformation is all wrong for it, and in my opinion they stand a good chance of injury. However, your Dane should not be asked to jump higher than 3 feet, the maximum set by The American Kennel Club and observed at all shows of member clubs.* I see no reason why they should not be allowed to jump a few feet to prove that out on a walk they can jump if you come to a fence or wall. You can, if you wish, omit the jumps and still qualify in obedience trials, but naturally you stand a better chance if the dog does jump.

The broad jump, however, can do little harm to any dog. It is taught by having flat slats of wood sloping toward the way of the approach and making them about ten inches high and 3 feet wide. Start the dog jumping about three of them on a lead with you jumping them with him; then stop yourself as he begins, and by using the word "jump" or "over," the dog is quickly taught. Eventually you may have the dog jumping 20 feet, which for a big dog is not too

---

*A dog may be expected to jump to a height of one and half times his own height at the withers, if this does not exceed 3 feet.

much, and which exceeds the Kennel Club maximum. My dog loves doing it. Smaller dogs jump 6 feet. It is useful when, out walking in the country, you have to jump a stream and, in my opinion, cannot injure the dog in any way. I do always wonder why in these trials such high marks are awarded for the jumps; I consider them a most unimportant part of obedience training.

Jumping Up. *I cannot cure my Labrador of jumping up at me and my visitors. It seems too cruel to hit her when she obviously is only showing us how much she loves us. What can I do to stop it?*

If you really object to this habit, you must stop your dog indulging in it. If she has been trained to obey the command "Sit" or "Down," tell her to sit as soon as you come into the room; you can then kneel down and caress her to make things up to her. When your guests leave, make her stay to heel for a few seconds until she quiets down. If, however, she disobeys the command to stay down and continues to jump up, hold out the palm of your hand so that she will bump her nose against it, at the same time ordering her in a really thunderous voice to get down. A dog's nose is very sensitive—she will not deliberately court many such bumps.

Kennel Club. *I am an overseas visitor to England and am most interested in your Kennel Club and its work for pedigreed-dog showing. Can you tell me something of its activities?*

The Kennel Club was founded in 1873 by S.E. Shirley, M.P., whose main interest was in Retrievers. At this time dog breeding and dog showing were on a par with horse coping and were not very respectable occupations, certainly not ones that any lady would have wanted to be connected with under any circumstances. Mr. Shirley decided to found a club on the lines of the Jockey Club, which governs all racing matters. He started with two rooms to work in and twelve basic rules for the running of shows and the registration of pedigreed dogs. His intention was to make this activity fit for all to partake in and enjoy.

By 1900 the Kennel Club was well established, and the Championship shows and the system of registration of dogs were run on the same lines as they are today. Kennel Clubs in other parts of the world were basing their organizations on the English pattern. Dog showing was fast becoming the respectable business it is today and the words "sold a pup" were not in such wide use as formerly. The idea that dog breeding and showing could be an occupation or hobby for the highest in the land as well as the more humble was well on the way, and the hallmark of respectability was added when Queen Victoria became the Kennel Club's patron, as have successive monarchs since then. By 1900 half the exhibitors were women; formerly only men took part in shows. Now the organization is vast. Every decade the registrations are doubled.

The Kennel Club regulations govern all dog shows from the village fete (unless it has less than four classes for pedigreed dogs, in which case it gets exemption from the rules) to the Championship shows like Cruft's, which attracts from all over the world people interested in dogs to its annual shows. The cream of the pedigreed dogs can be seen here. This show was started by Charles Cruft, who died in 1938; his widow handed the running of the show over to the Kennel Club during World War II. The Kennel Club also runs field trials for gundogs, and obedience shows and trials for all dogs.

One in twenty-five of all dogs registered are exported; many of these fetch large sums of money. £1,000 is not an unusual price.

The Kennel Club has recently moved to new quarters, as the old ones in Piccadilly were getting too cramped. In the new home there are facilities for meetings, and about one hundred of these are held every year. The registration of specialist clubs now tops the 1,000 mark, of which 500 are local canine societies, 300 specialist clubs, and 200 training clubs; the last of these are increasing rapidly as the vogue for training dogs gains momentum.

The club is run by a committee, one-third of whom retire each year. There is a club tie in two shades of green.

A copy of the Kennel Club show regulations may be obtained by applying to the Secretary of the Kennel Club, 1-4 Clarges Street, London, W.I., England.

* * *

I will let The American Kennel Club speak for itself:

Established September 17, 1884, the American Kennel Club is a non-profit organization devoted to the Advancement of pure-bred dogs. Its membership is comprised of more than 380 autonomous dog clubs throughout the United States. Each club's voting privileges can be exercised by a representative known as a "delegate." The delegates are the legislative body of the club, making the rules and electing directors from among their number. The management of the club's affairs is in the hands of the Board of Directors, whose responsibility it is to make regulations and policies in conformity with the rules.

Among the functions of the AKC are: to register pure-bred dogs, maintain a *Stud Book* and to publish a *Stud Book Register*; to adopt uniform rules governing dog shows, obedience trials and field trials and to maintain and publish the results of these events; and to publish a magazine—*Pure-Bred Dogs—American Kennel Gazette;* and generally to do everything possible to advance the development and interest in pure-bred dogs.

In 1971, AKC registered 1,129,200 dogs. During the same year, AKC approved 1232 dog shows in which 657,247 dogs competed; 735 obedience trials with 63,506 dogs competing; and 941 field trials with 108,976 dogs competing.

The *Stud Book*—the ancestry record of every dog that has been registered since the inception of The

American Kennel Club—now represents an enrollment of more than 15,000,000 dogs.

The *Stud Book Register*, a publication of The American Kennel Club, publishes in each monthly issue the sire and dam of each dog that has sired or whelped a litter if not previously published.

Pure-Bred Dogs—American Kennel Gazette is also published monthly. Each issue contains news of the various breed clubs, a list of forthcoming events that have been approved to be held under American Kennel Club rules, identification of those dogs that have finished their championships, the awards at all dog shows, obedience trials and field trials, as well as the "Secretary's Page," which contains actions taken by the club's Board of Directors.

The standards which govern the judging of all breeds eligible for show competition are published in *The Complete Dog Book*. The book also contains, in separate sections, breed histories, breed photographs, authoritative information on basic obedience training, as well as the breeding, care, and feeding of dogs.

The American Kennel Club maintains a reference library of 9,750 volumes on the dog. One of the most complete collections of its kind in the world, the library contains many rare, out-of-print editions; books and magazines in English and practically all foreign languages, some published as early as 1576; also the works of modern authorities on the breeds, and the stud books of other accredited registration agencies here and abroad. Included in the collection are famous prints and oil paintings by old masters and modern artists, as well as a unique file of pictures for the study of every known breed of dog. The public is invited to use the facilities of the library, which is open for reference purposes Mondays through Fridays from 10:00 A.M. to 4:00 P.M.

The American Kennel Club maintains an Information Service designed to assist breeders, dog owners and potential dog owners and to handle inquiries concerning any of the 116 breeds which are registrable in the AKC's *Stud Book*.

The address of The American Kennel Club is 51 Madison Avenue, New York, N.Y. 10010.

Kennels and Bedding. *I am buying a dog shortly and would*

be grateful for some advice as to whether I should buy a
kennel for him or keep him in the house. I have a part-time
job, which means that the dog must be alone from 8:00
A.M. until 2:00 P.M. every day.

The problem of the owner who has a job is always a difficult one, as it seems unfair to a dog lover to deny him or her the love and companionship of a dog under these circumstances. The life of an only dog is something like that of an only child, and I always ask the future owner if it would not be possible to keep two dogs as companions for each other. Under these circumstances I feel a kennel where the dogs could play together would be ideal. If, on the other hand, it is only possible to have one dog and that dog is kept in the house, the problem arises of what happens if the poor dog has a tummy upset and cannot get out to relieve itself when the owner is not there. A house-trained dog suffers tortures of remorse when this happens. If, on the other hand, this happens to a kennel dog, the run will undoubtedly be used and no harm done.

I think the construction of the kennel matters a lot. The most perfect range of kennels I ever saw were at the Guide Dogs for the Blind Association's place at Exford, England. Two dogs shared each kennel where this was possible, and they had a raised bench to sleep on. Ventilation was provided by grating as well as door and window, and they had a lovely concrete run. The doors were sheet-metal lined to save them from being gnawed. This kind of thing is obviously beyond the average owner's pocket, but a vast number of manufacturers of kennels do produce a great variety of types, with a considerable price range. I noticed one the other day that was 6 x 3 feet in area with bedroom and run, the sleeping quarters having a half-type stable door and the run a door in one piece. Of course kennel accommodation depends on the breed of dog you want. A German Shepherd, for example, has a weatherproof coat and can stand cold weather as long as he is dry and out of drafts, whereas a short-coated dog suffers if not kept much warmer.

Naturally guard duties are better performed by a dog kept indoors, and few burglars will burgle a house if they know a large or medium-sized dog is kept there.

If you decide to keep your dog in the house, let him get used to sleeping in the kitchen or somewhere where there is a tiled or linoleum floor. If he does this, and then, owing to tummy trouble, there is an accident, you will not feel like murder. A house-trained dog should never be scolded for an accident he could not help because nobody was there to let him out.

If the owner of a dog has to be away most of the day, the dog must have an outside kennel and be exercised before the owner leaves in the morning and after he comes home at night. Some people think such an arrangement cruel, but dogs soon get accustomed to routine, and hundreds of show dogs live this life. The dog should come into his own at the weekends if he can be with the owner most of the day, especially if he is allowed in the house.

Speaking of kennels, one must not forget the bedding of dogs. I have already mentioned that the sleeping bench should be raised off the floor, but the bench should also have a nice bed of clean wheat straw—never barley straw, because that has horrible awns that work into the dog's coat, eyes, and ears. Oat straw is only second best to wheat because it breaks up very quickly and is wasteful. Naturally dogs really love hay best because it keeps them so warm and cozy, but unless you are one of those energetic people who pick up long grass cuttings and dry them in the backyard, you may have to do without; even if you don't mind paying for hay, you may have no place to store it.

If the dog is kenneled, he is unlikely to be house-trained, so the kennel will have to be cleaned once a day and scrubbed with disinfectant once a week. Be sure it is perfectly dry before putting the dog back. The bench should not need scrubbing except perhaps in summer. I am assuming your dog is kept free from insects by either washing in a good dog soap or by being dusted or sprayed with an insecticide for dogs, which can be bought at any druggist, pet shop, or pet department. It is quite a good plan to dust a little of this powder on his bench occasionally and then brush it away some hours later. If there are any unwelcome insects in the vicinity, they will soon die. Kennel dogs should always be regularly examined for insects; it is amazing how they pick them up if you are not careful.

Kidney Trouble. *My dog seems to be drinking an awful lot of water, and I am frightened that he has kidney trouble. Can you explain a little about kidneys and what I should know as an amateur dog-owner?*

If you were to read about kidneys in a veterinary book, you would probably become very little the wiser. It is quite a complex subject. Roughly speaking, however, the kidneys are in the body to excrete urine and to act as selective filters, allowing only the passage of the water and salts and keeping back albumen and sugar. If the dog eats something like moldy dog biscuits, this may set up congestion of the kidneys, and the kidneys have to work overtime passing urine, trying to relieve the congestion. This congestion can be caused by a bacterial infection, but the resulting excessive passage of urine is nearly the same. Antibiotics form part of the treatment. Warmth, a laxative, easily digested food, and barley water all give the kidneys the rest they need to return to normal.

Kidney trouble should never be taken lightly, and professional advice should be sought early. It is because it is so important that I have asked a vet to write on this subject at some length:

Several diseases of an infectious nature affect primarily the liver or the kidneys of the dog.

1. *Infectious virus hepatitis* (Rhubarth's disease). Although this condition is caused by a virus, it does not seem to be as readily infectious, even in kennels, as one might expect. This may possibly be because some dogs are infected but the disease in them is so mild that it passes unnoticed. Other animals may show almost any signs from a slight passing illness to the acute disease with death in a few hours or days. In the mild form diagnosis is extremely difficult but in the more acute types the animal becomes very depressed, has a rise in temperature, increasing thirst, vomiting, and pain in the forward part of the floor of the abdomen. Food is usually refused and diarrhea may occur; the vomit is usually yellow and bile-stained, and the animal becomes increasingly dehydrated. In the most acute forms so much damage is done to the liver that death occurs rapidly.

2. *Leptospirosis.* There are two types of this disease. The first is caused by the organism called Leptospira icterohemorrhagica, most commonly called "jaundice" or "the yellows." This germ primarily affects the liver and the inflammation in that organ prevents the natural release of bile. It is bile circulating in the blood which causes the yellow discoloration which is such a marked symptom in the later stages of the disease. The animal loses its appetite, becomes very depressed, and frequently runs a high temperature. Vomiting is fairly frequent, at first white, then yellow. After a while yellow discoloration begins to appear and is most noticeable in the white of the eye and the gums. In light-colored dogs the skin of the abdomen is also noticeably yellow. All food is refused and there is usually an increased thirst, the animal vomiting up everything it drinks within a few moments. Depression is marked, dehydration occurs rapidly and is followed by death, in extreme cases, five or six days after the onset of symptoms. The trained observer will notice that the membranes of the eyes and mouth become dark and congested before the yellow discoloration appears. Treatment in these cases again consists of good nursing. Warmth and repeated small doses of fluids, preferably with glucose, are essential. A serum is available and antibiotics (penicillin, streptomycin, etc.) are also of value. A preventive vaccine is also available and may be used any time after four months of age. This particular germ affects

many different animals including, occasionally, man, and the common rat is the usual cause of spread. The germs are excreted in the saliva and the urine.

The second is Leptospira canicola. This germ is closely related to the one causing jaundice but it usually causes an inflammation of the kidneys (nephritis) of varying severity. It is known that very many dogs are infected, often without showing signs of illness but leaving the kidneys affected, which is probably the reason why chronic nephritis is one of the commonest causes of death in the older male dog. Frequently, however, the disease causes varying degrees of illness. The symptoms may vary considerably, but there is usually a rise in temperature and a loss of appetite, vomiting, and diarrhea. Pain is usually present in the kidney region and membranes may become congested at first, and later rather pale with, sometimes, very small hemorrhages on the gums. The breath becomes very unpleasant and the teeth sometimes stained. A very good percentage of cases recover if professional help is sought in time.

Lead Poisoning. *My puppy has eaten a lot of white paint off our doors. I have been told he may die from lead poisoning. Is this true?*

I think your puppy would be dead already if he had eaten enough of this white paint. Lead poisoning builds up until it becomes fatal. Never let a puppy chew anything with any paint on it, whether it be dangerous like lead paint or just ordinary paint without lead in its makeup. If you know your puppy has had a lot of lead paint, immediately give him, as a first-aid precaution, milk and the whites of one or two eggs.

The treatment of poisoning of all kinds must be based on knowledge of the antidote. For example, if the puppy has eaten rat poison containing phosphorus, on no account give eggs, oil, fats, or milk, as they render the phosphorus more soluble and therefore more dangerous. Try to make the dog sick by pushing your finger down its throat, and give barley water if available. I shall not give a list of antidotes because few households have them.

Limping. *My dog is limping on a front leg, yet I don't know of any injury she has sustained. Could it be rheumatism?*

Without seeing the dog or knowing her age, it is very difficult to say what the cause of lameness could be. But I have in past years met many dogs who suffered from slipped disks, a trouble so common among human beings today. It is difficult to diagnose because nothing seems to hurt the dog much when you are pressing and poking the lame leg. I have found that small dogs, if lifted up by their tails and given a little shake, walk perfectly soundly when I put them down again, and remain sound. This all points to disk trouble rather than rheumatism, especially if the dog is a young one. Owners very often notice this lameness after the dog has been having a rough and tumble with another dog, or turns suddenly while chasing a ball. All this would point to a slipped disk.

It is, however, essential to examine the dog's paws very closely for a thorn or a tiny cut. This is done more easily when the paw is wet. The hair then lies flat and the thorn can be seen more readily. It could also be a sprain, which can be diagnosed by swelling, pain, and local heat.

These are only first-aid suggestions, for I feel sure that an owner would consult a vet if the lameness were severe or lasting.

Listlessness. *My dog, at three years old, seems terribly listless. He comes for walks but drags behind all the time, and really doesn't seem to care whether he goes out or not. What can I do for him?*

I wonder how much fun his walks are in the first place. Dogs loathe shopping or the same walk every day—their tails drop with disappointment when they see where they are going. First of all, I should try training him daily in set exercises, following the schedule for beginners at obedience shows, then, after ten minutes a day of that, I should romp with him and praise him. I feel you yourself must be a bit dull with the dog to make him so uninterested in everything you do for him.

But, of course, there is always the chance that the dog is not well. I should put him on a course of vitamins, especially vitamin B complex, which includes all the necessary vitamin B for the dog's health. Make sure his digestion is in order, by giving him a course of vitamins A and C. It may be that you are not feeding him correctly. If he is not having raw meat, put him on to raw meat only for about a week. Sometimes dogs' tummies seem to get tired of the usual diet, and a complete change and sometimes a day without food makes them feel much better.

Some dogs are very quiet by nature, and all they seem to want to do is sleep. Many people who own restless dogs like Boxers and Terriers would give anything to have a little of that trait in their pets!

Sometimes dogs that have been overtrained become dull and listless: all the naughtiness seems to have been taken out of them, and they don't wish to do anything that gets them into trouble. Be sure you only train your dog enough to make it well behaved. Some people get the obedience germ to such an extent that their dogs are slaves to their ambitions in this field. If this is the case, do no obedience training for six months, and you will find a vast improvement in your dog.

Monorchids and Cryptorchids. *What are monorchids and cryptorchids? I am always hearing these words in show circles and hate to admit my ignorance.*

They are words used for male dogs whose testicles have not descended normally. Monorchid means that only one testicle has descended into the scrotum, and cryptorchid means neither testicle has descended.

The American Kennel Club bars from show competition any dog that "does not have two normal testicles normally located in the scrotum." In my opinion, dogs with this defect are justifiably barred from the show ring.

A monorchid can still beget puppies, but both defects, in my opinion, make the dog a bad one for it may have a very uncertain temperament. I find them extremely difficult to train. I recommend castration, which is more difficult than usual as the undescended testicle has to be found before the operation of castration can be performed.

Inexperienced dog buyers may buy one of these and get badly bitten as they are usually appalling fighters as well as ineligible for shows. In fact I can see nothing to recommend keeping one. There has even been much ill feeling in the past when English breeders have sold these defective animals to go abroad. The Kennel Club of England has now taken steps to protect buyers of exported dogs.

Nails. *What care should I give my dog's nails?*

Most dogs who get regular road exercise need little attention to their nails, but dogs who get little exercise or who exercise mostly on grass do need them cut about once a month. This cutting should either be done by an expert or at home with proper nail clippers. It should never be attempted with scissors. The nail might break and cause severe pain to the dog.

The length of nail varies considerably according to the breed and also among dogs of a particular breed. I own a Miniature Black-and-Tan Terrier that has never been able to have her nails cut. I only tried once and hurt the quick, though the nail looked as if it needed cutting. These nails have never grown any longer in five years, yet her companion, my Great Dane Juno, has her nails cut every three weeks. They both have the same amount of exercise.

When the nails are white, the quick can be easily seen and the nail can be then cut to about one-sixth of an inch off the quick. If the dog flinches, don't cut it so short. If a dog should break or split a nail, wrap the nail round with adhesive bandage, and it will soon be all right again.

Nettle Rash. *My dog suddenly came out in a nettle rash. What should I have done?*

Nettle rash is usually an allergy to something the dog has eaten. The cure is to give antihistamine products either by mouth, by injection, or locally in the form of cream. Local applications of double-strength calamine lotion cool the spots and make the dog more comfortable.

Noise, Sensitiveness to. *My dog is terrified of noise from airplanes, thunder, guns, etc. What can I do to help him, as I live in an area where these things are a common nuisance?*

Under no circumstances whatever, sympathize with your dog; this only makes him worse. Let loud noises form part of your playing together: make him learn a game in which he pretends to attack you while you fire a gun with caps in it. Make him get excited every time you hear a bang of any sort. Be sure to take him in the traffic and among people everywhere as often as possible. Sedatives do help around the Fourth of July, but they are not a cure. The cure is to establish an association of ideas in your dog's mind between noise and enjoyable games.

Noses. *My dog often gets a hot nose, yet he seems perfectly well. I thought dogs should have cold noses at all times. Is this so?*

A dry nose is not always the indication of fever. I once knew an Irish Setter in excellent health who, after he had recovered from hard pad, never had a wet, cold nose, but I would always be suspicious that he had or was developing something like kidney trouble that was causing him to lose the fluid normally excreted by the sweat glands of the nose. Take the dog's temperature. If it is normal, that is, $101.5°$ F. taken in the bowel, if the dog shows no symptoms of diarrhea or excessive drinking and passing of urine, and is gay and willing to go for walks, I should not worry overmuch.

Lack of water can of course cause a dry nose; most dogs have dry noses when they have been asleep, but as soon as they get up and about, the nose becomes normal again.

Obedience Training. *I have heard so much about obedience training classes for dogs. Can you give me some information about what goes on?*

Obedience classes are springing up all over the country. It is quite the thing to attend one these days, and no shame is attached to owners who cannot train their own dogs. But there are good schools and bad schools with efficient or inefficient instructors. Unfortunately beginners do not know the difference, and much harm is done by bad training and by owners who then go about saying that training is no good. Some people think any sort of training is better than no training at all. I do not agree. I think trainers should only be allowed to register the clubs they run when they have passed a certain standard of efficiency, rather like the L drivers (learners) on the road. But this will never come; many people would say it was a restriction of liberty. I, however, handle many dogs in a year that have been allegedly trained by others, and I find them much more difficult to handle than absolute novices; for they have learned how to counteract training, their muscles become tensed when they know you want to put them to the "down," for example, and they are often ready to bite. Recently I was asked for advice about a German Shepherd that had been to another trainer's class and had bitten the trainer, who reacted by promptly banning that dog from further classes instead of being all the keener to tackle him for the unfortunate owner. If you are afraid of dogs, you will make a hopeless trainer, for dogs know who fears them. A list of training clubs registered with the Kennel Club can be got from there. You will probably be put into the beginners' class, unless you happen to attend classes in which beginners are not segregated. My own clubs are nongraded. I believe beginners only stay beginners for about five minutes, when their dogs are capable of joining in all the exercises the more experienced dogs work on. By working with good dogs and experienced handlers, the beginner and his dog are not so muddled for they can watch the others. When all are beginners, everyone is making mistakes, so watching the others is useless.

The fee varies according to the type of school or club. Some schools offer private instruction, which is, of course, more expensive. Most schools charge one fee for the entire training course.

Most schools and clubs run competitions for their members; progress is noted, and novices are graded up to different classes. Choke chains of one sort or another are standard equipment and can usually be bought at the school or club, which buys them in quantity and gets them cheaply.

Obstinacy. *My dog is terribly obstinate. I have studied training methods and try jerking the dog on a choke chain when he wants to fight other dogs or pulls on the lead. The result is that I hurt my back and he stays victorious. How can I break this obstinacy?*

You forgot to mention what type of dog you find so stubborn but, whatever the type, it is obviously beyond your strength to handle him. For with a dog lacking in sensitivity the cure is strength on the part of the handler, an iron will to succeed, and daily training for half an hour. If possible, get a strong man to give the initial jerks. When jerking a dog that pulls on the lead, so many people jerk in an upward direction instead of down and back behind the knee. One way is effective, the other useless. Be sure you have the right type of thick-linked choke chain; I suspect you have a fine-linked one, which is absolutely useless for this type of dog. You must also praise the dog a lot; he does not sound as if he had much affection for you. Castrate him if necessary to stop his interest in other dogs. Only by perseverance will you make this dog obedient. Some dogs are so mad as to be untrainable, and they are best put away. No dog can be a pleasure if he is uncontrollable.

Odors. *My dog smells bad and also makes odors when he is asleep. Can you help me cure him?*

Have you examined his teeth? Although dogs are not very prone to have caries or holes in their teeth, it is possible, and badly decayed teeth can make a dog's mouth smell. Also, do you wash your dog's mouth occasionally? Think of all the food, and dirty things as well, that he touches with his lips. The liquid from overfull anal glands makes a dog smell terribly. If this is the cause, get them squeezed by a vet. Flatulence is caused by a too fatty diet; correct this and one source of doggy odors is dispelled. Urine from a male dog makes more of a smell than that from a bitch; wash the dog in a good dog soap, and that particular smell will go.

Vitamin A in large doses for a few weeks helps digestion and reduces the risk of bowel flatulence. Discharge of any sort from the vagina of a bitch smells horrid and needs instant attention. It might be the start of pyometra or inflammation in the womb.

Certain skin diseases like mange have a horrible smell. Examine the dog for any bare patches if this is found to be the cause.

Old Age and Its Diseases. *I dread the day when my dog will be no more. How long can healthy dogs be expected to live?*

The answer to this question depends on so many things; the home the dog lives in, and whether he is fed on a sensible diet, given proper exercise, and kept reasonably slim. It also depends on the size of the dog. Small dogs live longer than large breeds. For example, a Great Dane's life is not usually much longer than ten or eleven years, whereas I have known a Manchester Terrier that was eighteen years old. My neighbor's Fox Terrier is already thirteen but full of beans. Normally, though, I think that if a dog reaches the age of twelve, he has nearly had his span of life.

Remember, dogs need less exercise as they get older, and much less food. They sleep for long periods at a time, and the owner should no longer force the dog to go for long walks when it seems disinclined to do so. With bitches, watch carefully the heat period and make sure they have no evil-smelling discharge. Pyometra is very common in aged bitches and can be fatal. Pyometra is an inflammation of the womb; pus gets locked up inside and causes acute infection if not dealt with either by antibiotics, or in many cases the operation for removal of the female organs that is known as partial or complete hysterectomy according to the organs removed.

As a precaution I always put my own bitch on antibiotics for three days after her heat is finished. Before I did this, she was always dull and listless and obviously not well, although nothing like an emergency flared up. Now she returns to her old self very quickly.

Many people ask me when bitches stop coming in heat. The answer is that they don't have a menopause as we know it, and heat continues as long as the bitch lives. That does not, of course, mean they are always capable of breeding; very often they refuse to produce puppies some years before they are really old.

One should watch for blindness and deafness in old dogs. I know several people who keep dogs whose sight has almost entirely gone. Whether this is cruelty or kindness is a point for discussion, but I think it is cruel. I think in most cases the owner lacks the courage to put the pet to sleep. In my opinion, deafness is not in the same category; I have trained a few dogs deaf from birth and found them quite trainable and able to enjoy life like normal dogs. If this is the only disability the aging dog suffers from, I feel it is not a bad one.

Some dogs, as they get old, get incontinent and get sore from urine perpetually dripping over their hindquarters. This is unpleasant for both owner and dog and, after seeking professional advice as to whether any treatment will cure this trouble and finding the answer to be negative, I think the animal should be put to sleep. Such dogs cannot sleep in the house without constant change of bedding, and even the smell is horrid. They drink excessive amounts of water, which usually denotes kidney failure, and altogether the dog's life cannot be a very happy one.

Ownership, Obligations of. *I am a very busy person, and have no time to exercise my dog. He goes off a lot on his own but always comes back for his meals. People say I should not allow this, but how else is the poor dog to get any exercise?*

I nearly had apoplexy when I read your letter. You are one of the selfish dog-owners who cause all us other poor dog-owners such trouble. You are one of the brigade who are the cause of so much death and danger on the roads. You are guilty of allowing your dog to be a pest to owners of bitches around whose homes they swarm. You don't even love your dog enough to care whether he gets killed or injured when he is out on these sprees! You are utterly unthinking and selfish and should never own a dog at all.

If you keep a dog, you owe him care and affection. You should see he is a danger to no one, and you should exercise him yourself. I fail to understand what pleasure this dog can be to you except perhaps as guardian of your property at night. I sincerely hope that, after reading my reply, you have the decency to mend your ways, so that you and your dog may become respectable members of the community.

Panting. *Why do dogs pant?*

Unlike horses, dogs do not sweat through the skin; they sweat through the tongue and nose, so that when a dog is panting, he is not necessarily thirsty. He is just sweating. Naturally if exertion makes a dog pant for long, he loses fluid, which he will have to replace by drinking water. Panting does not necessarily mean thirst, but a thirsty dog will pant.

Excessive panting may indicate distress, and dogs should be taken into a shady or cool place or they may get a heatstroke. It is not unknown for dogs to die at shows in hot weather from heatstroke. If a stroke is threatened, immediately put cold compresses to the dog's head or, if the temperature is extremely high, immerse the dog in cold water until the temperature is reduced to about 103°, which is fairly safe for a dog. Of course the animal must be dried off, or chill may result. If the animal has not lost consciousness, cool drinks are invaluable. Shutting dogs in cars with the windows closed is one cause of heatstroke. Only thoughtless owners would do such a thing.

Paraphimosis. *The other day my Pug dog seemed to be having trouble with his penis. He got very excited over a bitch, and I think his penis protruded from its sheath and would not go back in. I was terribly worried, though it did right itself eventually. What is the cause of this, and what should I have done?*

This occurrence is fairly common in male dogs. It is termed paraphimosis and occurs more in small dogs than large ones. It is caused by the orifice of the sheath being rather small and contracting on the penis when this has protruded; the latter then becomes swollen and painful and cannot be retracted without help. If not noticed early, the point of the penis becomes much inflamed. The treatment should be to try and ease the sheath over the penis again; if necessary, put a little medicinal paraffin oil on the penis to lubricate it. If the dog will allow it, ice helps to reduce the swelling. The dog should be lying on his back or side when you carry out this treatment.

If all first aid fails, the vet may have to make a snip in the prepuce to allow the penis to retract.

Pneumonia. *Please give me details of how to recognize pneumonia and of what treatment I should give. I lost my Peke years ago from this, and now with a new puppy I should like to be wise early.*

You are naturally nervous about this trouble arising again, but nowadays antibiotics have made pneumonia a far less dangerous condition than it was. It is not common in dogs, usually occurring only as a complication after some other disease, like hard pad or distemper. But it can develop as a secondary infection after an accident or even from a common cold, if the dog is allowed to get chilled or wet.

The symptoms are shivering and a rising temperature, which may reach 104° or even more. Respirations are rapid and painful and, if you have any experience of these things, place your ear against the dog's ribs behind the front leg, where you will hear a grating inspiration and expiration. It takes experience to recognize these sounds, though, and in any case the owner of a dog affected by pneumonia would be well advised to get professional advice. In pneumonia the dog usually stays lying on his side.

The first thing to do is to make the dog a pneumonia jacket, and you can buy gauze-covered cotton for this from any druggist. Make a hole for the head and front paws, and then sew tapes on to keep it in place.

The whole treatment of pneumonia depends on the use

of antibiotics and on keeping the dog warm while allowing him fresh air to help his breathing. The dog's appetite will be bad, and light nourishing food should be given. The bowels should be kept in a laxative state; give a purge at first and then liquid medicinal paraffin.

The drugs needed for the treatment of pneumonia cannot be obtained by the ordinary owner; it is essential to employ a vet to handle the case as soon as possible.

Professional Trainers. *My dog is extremely willful. Can you take him to train for me?*

I am afraid that if I took your dog and trained him for you, you would not be at all pleased with the result when you got him home, for you would not find him much improved. The reason is that I seldom have any trouble with any dog, which sounds like boasting but really means that I understand dogs and intend to stand no nonsense from disobedient ones. This the naughty dog senses at my approach and behaves himself. But you obviously haven't that way with dogs as you find your dog willful. All dogs and children can be extremely willful if you allow them to get away with it. Different owners have vastly different characters, and even in your own home you may find that your dog obeys your husband, or even one of your children, but won't obey you. All this goes to show that it is the handler of the dog that needs the instruction more than the naughty dog.

You owe your dog something, and that something is to make him a pleasant companion at all times. This takes daily, firm, but loving training—insisting that he carry out your commands when you give them and never letting him get the better of you. If you fail, you must seek more experienced help. This can be got by reading books or by attending local classes. What you decide to do depends on your free time and purse, but it should not include sending your dog away to be trained by himself. You would be better off leaving your dog at home and going and watching the training alone. There is a vast amount to be learned in this dog-training game. I genuinely believe dogs are becoming more difficult to handle owing to bad temperaments deriving from indiscriminate breeding. I get over 10,000 letters a year from owners of naughty dogs, so I think I can say I have considerable experience of this problem.

Public Transport. *I want to take my dog on a railway journey with me. What are the regulations governing train travel for dogs?*

Normally dogs can travel only in the baggage cars on American passenger trains. Exceptions are commuter lines operating out of large cities. These trains rarely have baggage cars, which means that they cannot accommodate large dogs. Small dogs, kept in portable kennels, can accompany their owners if they don't obstruct or annoy the other passengers. Actually, this leaves quite a lot to the discretion of the conductor, who may, or may not, be a dog lover.

Another exception is made for passengers with rooms or roomettes; they can keep their dogs with them. Otherwise it's the baggage car, where the dog must be confined in a crate labeled with the owner's name, address, and destination. The passenger is responsible for his pet's care, though sometimes a kindly baggage attendant will let the dog out of the crate for a while—he may be more likely to do this if the dog is muzzled.

The charge for a dog is 21% of the passenger's one-way fare, and the dog is automatically insured for $25. The railroad will sell additional insurance on a dog to a $200 maximum.

The great trouble about traveling with a dog on a long journey is the lack of time at stopping places to exercise him; therefore traveling by night is best for him when he is accustomed to sleeping anyway without relieving himself. If traveling on a long-distance train with your dog, be sure to

take adequate food, and a bowl for water. Food for dogs is
not obtainable on trains. I always take a rug for the dog to
lie on as well.

For long trips, air travel is kinder in that the travel time
is so very much shorter. Small dogs in carriers can generally
be kept at the owner's seat, as long as the other passengers
don't object. Large dogs must travel as baggage. Carriers can
be purchased from the airlines. Take along a drill so that
you can make extra holes in the carriers; they should have
air holes on four sides, top, and bottom—this last to let
heavier-than-air gases escape. Be sure to specify that you
want your dog to travel in a vented pet cargo bin.

Some airlines, American Airlines for one, figure the price
at twice the excess baggage rate. Costs vary greatly from one
airline to another.

Nowadays there are specialists whose job it is to arrange
transport for dogs by land, sea, and air. Look under the
heading "Pet Transporting" in your telephone book yellow
pages. These firms can save you a great deal of worry.

Pulse Rate. *What is the normal pulse rate in a dog?*

The pulse rate varies according to the size of the dog; a
small breed may have a pulse rate of 100 beats a minute
while that of a Great Dane is usually only about 70. The
beat is often intermittent, so do not rush to the vet if that
seems all that is wrong with your dog.

In cases of illness the pulse rate increases to anything up
to about 150 to 160 beats per minute in a small dog and
about 100 or slightly more in a big dog. A slow pulse is
more dangerous than a fast one as it often means collapse of
the patient. In pneumonia the pulse rate is often slow
because the heart is affected. Naturally after exertion the
rate is fast, but it should return to normal within a few
minutes of rest. If the pulse is very weak or slow, give
stimulants. It is best felt on the inside of the dog's thigh

where the big femoral artery is superficial and easily contacted, or the inside of the forearm. You must move your
fingers over the area to find its position. Take the pulse with
your fingers, not your thumb, or you may be taking your
own pulse and not that of the dog.

Vets often go more by the type of pulse felt than the
speed, because naturally any dog excited at being handled
by a stranger may have a faster than normal pulse.

Quarantine. *I live in the United States and want to return
to England next spring, but I have a Collie who has been my
constant pal for eight years. It would break his heart to go
into quarantine. Is there any way I can have him quaran-
tined at my home?*

This is a terrible thing for all owners of well-loved dogs
who wish to leave England temporarily and take their pets,
and especially for blind people who depend entirely on their
guide dogs to get around, but I am afraid the Ministry of
Agriculture is absolutely unrelenting. No appeal from anyone asking to be allowed to bring a dog into England
without quarantining it at a recognized place can be enter-
tained. Private vets, if they comply with the regulations, can
be recognized as suitable people to have dogs in quarantine,
but very few take advantage of it. The rules are so terribly
stringent! I am sure every owner of a beloved dog has at one
time or another tried to think out a scheme for smuggling a
dog into this country without anyone knowing, but although it has been done in the past and probably will be
done again, it is simply not worth it. I am sure no one who has
seen rabies either in a dog or a human being would for one
moment contemplate such action. It is quite the most
terrible of diseases, and the stringent rules in Britain do
make sure that there is no risk of dogs' bringing it in. I get
many thousands of letters a year from dog-owners whose
dogs bite them; at least they know those dogs are not
affected with rabies, however mad they seem! I think, if

your dog has to go into quarantine rather than be put to sleep before leaving another country to enter this one, you should try and quarantine him somewhere where you can visit him daily. Dogs soon learn to rely on the owner's visits, and I have known several desperately worried owners who did this and found their dogs quickly settled down. I know there have been outbreaks of such diseases as hard pad in quarantine kennels, but if you have your dog inoculated against as many things as you can, the risk is not very great. Only dog lovers would take up this work of being with dogs in quarantine, and I feel sure they do everything in their power to make dogs happy. I left my own bitch behind when I left the Argentine, hoping to return shortly. As it turned out, I never went back. I never knew what happened to my dog, as the man who had promised to put her to sleep if I didn't return gave her away instead. I never forgave myself for trusting him. I feel sure, if you really believe as I did, that a dog will not survive quarantine, it is better to put the dog to sleep and know his end.

The quarantine period is twelve months, but as there are on record cases of rabies having developed after that time, it is not by any means too long a time to isolate the dog.

The only dogs that escape being put into quarantine kennels are dogs taking part in a performing act. These dogs are allowed out of their kennels for their specific act and are then immediately put back in their locked kennels. It is a horrible life for any dog, but as they only come from abroad for a short time, they just have to put up with it. The regulations certainly keep dog-owners from taking their holidays abroad if they are not willing to put them into boarding kennels or a friend's care for the time they are away.

The United States is less stringent about dogs entering the country. A certificate of rabies vaccination is required for a dog unless it is coming directly from Australia, the Bahamas, Bermuda, Denmark, Fiji, Iceland, Ireland, Jamaica, New Zealand, Norway, Sweden, or the United Kingdom of Great Britain. The requirements are based on the incidence of rabies in the locality a dog comes from, and additional safeguards can be employed if the medical officer finds an animal suspect. The rabies inoculation certificate, which identifies the dog and is signed by a licensed veterinarian, must be dated thirty days before entry and must specify whether the dog was vaccinated with "nervous-tissue" vaccine or with chicken-embryo vaccine. The former is officially deemed effective for one year; the latter, for three years. Confinement is required for one month following vaccinations; this is applied chiefly in two situations: when dogs arrive without valid certificates of vaccination, and in the case of puppies less than three months old (here the owner must certify that the puppy will be vaccinated at three months old and suitably confined).

Rabbits, as Food. *A friend of mine always feeds her Labradors on whole rabbits, skin, bones and all. Isn't this a very risky thing to do?*

It is a natural thing to do, and the owner is only following nature's pattern for the complete nourishment of the dog. But, in my opinion, Mother Nature can do very silly things, and everyone knows that rabbit or chicken bones can choke a dog or perforate the intestine. Therefore, I think it is risky. Rabbit is an excellent change of diet from beef for dogs, and the livers are particularly relished. But always be sure that the livers are perfectly healthy before feeding them to dogs: rabbits can suffer from a disease called coccidiosis, which infects the liver and which can be detected as small white nodules on the liver. If these are seen, do not use the liver under any circumstances, as this infection can be caught by dogs, who then develop blood-stained diarrhea and become very ill. Moreover, rabbits frequently suffer from tapeworms, which can also be passed on to dogs with very harmful effects. If your friend allows her dogs to eat whole rabbits straight from the traps, how can she know they are not infected with disease?

Rats, as Disease Carriers. *I have heard that rats pass some disease on to dogs. What can I do to protect my dog, as I live in a thickly populated place, where rats might easily come across from the warehouses?*

Leptospira icterohemorrhagica (see p. 205) causes a disease that can be fatal to dogs and is passed from rats to dogs. Nowadays there is an inoculation to protect dogs against it, and owners would be well advised to take advantage of it. The symptoms resemble distemper at first, and owners may be confused. But as expert treatment with antibiotics is essential very quickly in either case, no sensible owner would hesitate to call in the vet.

Rickets. *What is rickets and what causes it? Do all puppies have rickets to begin with?*

Rickets is the result of nutritional deficiencies and of lack of fresh air and sunlight. It may be apparent in very young puppies if the mother has had insufficient nourishment of the right sort to be able to pass antirachitic substances like phosphorus, calcium, and vitamin D on to her unborn litter. Lack of liberty is a contributory factor, and seldom is rickets seen in puppies who play in sunlight. Nevertheless, it is always wise not only to give the mother plenty of vitamins A and D before the birth of the puppies but to commence adding cod-liver oil to the diet of the puppies as soon as weaning commences.

The symptoms are enlarged joints, "cow hocks" (which means the hocks nearly knock together when the puppy is walking), and potbelly (which can also be caused by worms). As the puppy becomes heavier, the front legs may bend with the weight of the body and the elbows just out so that the legs are bowed. The pasterns tend to bend over instead of being upright and strong, and the puppy is a sorry sight. In some cases lameness appears for no apparent reason. The treatment is sunlight, or ultraviolet rays if available, cod-liver oil, or the malt compounds that contain everything necessary to prevent or cure rickets. Give plenty of room to exercise, but not too much forced walking in the early stages of the treatment, worming, raw meat, milk, and extra calcium and phosphorus in capsule or liquid form. Nowadays no one should allow their puppies to suffer from rickets. Some people say the disease is hereditary. If that is the case, care is needed more than ever to ensure that the bitch is adequately supplied during pregnancy with all the necessary vitamins and minerals and that this treatment continues as weaning time begins.

Road Accidents. *What should I do if I am involved in an accident with a dog: (1) with regard to treatment of the injured dog, and (2) from the legal aspect?*

To get involved in an accident in which a dog is injured is a ghastly experience for anyone. It should be an offense to allow a dog to be unaccompanied on any highway.

Should you be on hand when one of these accidents occurs, remember that it may be extremely dangerous to move a badly injured dog. Unless it seriously interferes with traffic, leave it where it lies, but cover it up warmly to counteract shock. Stop any bleeding either by pressure at the bleeding point or on the artery supplying it. Get someone to call professional assistance immediately. If no one at hand knows the address of a vet, the police—or a telephone call to A.S.P.C.A.—will often help locate one. If the condition of the dog is obviously hopeless, the A.S.P.C.A. can destroy the animal to prevent further suffering. In any case, try to have the dog's owner located as soon as possible to take charge of the situation. Very often, however, these stray wanderers do not carry their owners' names and addresses on their collars, or their licenses.

In many states the law requires that a driver involved in an accident with a dog stop and give his name and address to the owner of the dog. If no owner is present, he must notify the police of the accident within twenty-four hours of its occurrence. In New York State a hit-and-run accident involving an animal is a misdemeanor. The driver is required to remain with the animal, wait for a law officer, and fill out an accident report. The animal's owner may sue the driver for the price of the animal.

Road Sense. *My dog is a jaywalker: he has no road sense whatsoever and would as soon walk under a car as wait. How can one teach a dog road sense?*

I don't think you need worry about teaching a dog road sense. I always feel that as long as the owner trains the dog to sit at every curb, not to pull him into the road, and not to attack other dogs, there should be no trouble because no dog should be off the lead in any road where there is likely to be traffic. Even my own dogs stay on their leads in the streets, and they have won dozens of prizes for obedience. You never know when something will distract the dog to the point of making him forget all road sense. Human beings forget and get killed, after all, and dogs have less than human intelligence. Guide dogs are taught road sense by constant practice in busy streets, and it takes extremely experienced trainers to carry out this training. With practice, your dog will eventually sit at every curb and connect an empty road with crossing in safety, but never rely on this. It is better to be safe than sorry.

Shows and Showing. *I have a very beautiful eight-month-old Sealyham puppy, which I would like to show. Can you give me any hints on how to handle him? I don't want to annoy the judge by appearing inept.*

This showing game is one of the most fascinating in the

world, but it can also be frustrating. You have to have the right attitude toward winning or losing or you will not last very long, but you have started on the right road by inquiring how to make the best of your dog at a show.

First of all, train him to walk or run on a loose lead, and by this I mean a lead at least 4 feet long, so that you can hold it well ahead of him and his action is not then spoiled by turning sideways toward you. He should be gay and happy but must not leap about or jump up. Nothing annoys a judge more than to see a top-class dog misbehaving and therefore not going to the top because it was impossible to see its action or faults properly. The dog should stand quite still on a loose lead. Some people may say the ordinary obedience training makes a dog sit and will not train their dogs for this reason. I say this is nonsense. If a dog is trained properly, it should stand on command as well as sit. To make a dog do this, every time you stop, run your hand under his tummy and scratch it with the command "Stand"; he loves the scratching and soon stands well waiting for it. If for some reason or other this doesn't work, hold a twig in your left hand and, as you stop, place it quietly under the dog's tummy. He will not sit on a twig and therefore remains standing. Next, get friends to walk around him; he should stand still. With Sealyhams most judges seem to allow the handler to hold the dog's head up tightly by its lead and to balance the tail upward also. To do this, you crouch at its side. But I think this is a sign that you have not trained your dog properly and I feel sure that one day this "stringing up" of show dogs will be forbidden. Always have something nice in your hand; if his ball makes him look alert, hold that. If an odd noise makes him look nice for a moment, make one, but the more naturally the dog looks alert the better. No one is allowed under Kennel Club rules to attract the dog's attention from outside the ring, but you can let someone else handle him and stand by the ringside yourself, which, if he loves you very much, will make him look alert seeking you out. This is not without risks though,

for if the judge notices it and construes it as double handling, can disqualify your dog. As a matter of fact, the judge
is the absolute authority at a show and can disqualify a dog
with little or no need to justify his decision.

Next, you must train your dog to be handled without
snapping or fidgeting. He must stand quite still when the
judge runs his hands over him, and must not sit as his back
is pressed. Small dogs will be placed on a table to be
handled, and I have found in the past that when a dog is
being appraised at a distance, he will stand very well if you
occasionally tickle his ribs at the side farthest away from
the judge; all dogs love this gentle scratching—it even stops
youngsters fidgeting. Stand him squarely on his hind legs,
not in an overstretched position but so that the hind leg
nearest the judge is farther back than its fellow. This gives
the judge an all-around view of the four legs. To get him to
stand square on his front legs, lift his head off the ground
by placing your hands on either side of his head and,
catching hold of either the collar or scruff, drop him squarely down on his legs. This gets him up on his toes and
prevents his legs turning in or out in an awkward position.

When the judge wishes to examine his teeth, open the
front of the dog's mouth (lips only) to show the bite with
the upper and lower teeth closed together. (If the judge
moves to open the dog's mouth himself, he is exercising his
prerogative, and he may be seriously annoyed at any interference on your part.) This tells the judge whether the dog
has a perfect mouth or whether he is undershot or overshot
in the jaw: if the upper set of teeth overlap the lower ones
too much, he is overshot; on the other hand, if the lower set
overlap the upper set, he is undershot, which is a bad fault.
The teeth should be clean and, if through illness or any
other cause, the teeth have become stained or covered with
tartar, they must be cleaned or scraped. But as this is an
experienced person's job, I should let the expert who trims
him for show deal with this.

This trimming of a Sealyham is a highly skilled job; you

can spoil his appearance and, temporarily, his coat by bad trimming. Before the show he should not be washed except for his legs and whiskers. He should be thoroughly cleaned with a block of whitening, and this powder must be brushed out before going into the ring or you will be breaking a Kennel Club rule.

The best way to learn about showing is to go and watch the experts before trying the game yourself. See how the champion is handled. Ask the breeders to give you tips. Most of them are delightful people, only too willing to help a novice. Some show people, however, seem unbelievably jealous or vicious—I have never decided which—and almost seem to be contemplating murder when a newcomer enters the game. Keep your distance from this type of person, who can spoil the show game; it may be a livelihood to them, but is probably only a hobby for you.

Be sure, before taking your dog to any show, to protect him by having him inoculated against hard pad and distemper. Shows can be hotbeds of disease if exhibitors don't take this precaution. Watch your dog carefully for at least ten days after the show in case he has picked up anything.

When you sign for entry in a show, your signature indicates that you know and acknowledge all American Kennel Club Rules and Regulations, as well as any additional requirements of the particular show you are entering.

Always be ready to appear in your class when it is called.

Some shows require a veterinarian's inspection. At such shows I never permit the vet to handle my dog's mouth; if he wants to see her tonsils, I open her mouth myself. I know the vets wash their hands, but as a doctor's wife I also know that the perfunctory washing possible between handling dogs is not sufficient to sterilize the hands. In fact I think this veterinary inspection should be abolished altogether and replaced by a vet's certificate brought after examination by a vet at the dog's home the previous day. But then I am full of reforms I would like brought in for the comfort and safety of dogs and exhibitors!

Always begin your showing career at small local shows until you have the hang of it; the judges at these shows are usually amateurs, who are much freer with advice than licensed judges. Professional judges are so often accused of favoritism that any advice or tips on showing they give might easily be misinterpreted. The camaraderie is good at small shows, and you and your dog won't have traveled too far and got too tired. If you win at a few small shows, it will egg you on to higher things.

Sick Nursing. *If my dog gets ill, is there anything special I should know about nursing him?*

Nursing animals is very similar to nursing human beings. The place where they are nursed should be kept warm yet airy; both heat and ventilation are important. The carpet should be protected or removed if the dog has bowel or kidney trouble or is likely to be sick.

Ample water should always be available unless the vet has forbidden it. A wool coat should be made for the dog if he has pneumonia, and provision for changing his bedding should also be made.

Sick dogs should not come in contact with any other dogs. Remember also that dogs do get tuberculosis, which is highly dangerous to human beings; if this is suspected, call in the vet and, if its presence is proved, destroy the dog immediately. Tuberculosis is one of the few diseases for which such measures are still necessary.

Nowadays antibiotics coupled with efficient nursing bring about recoveries in cases where no hope would have been held out fifty years ago.

The diet should be attractive to the dog, but remember that the patient is not taking his usual exercise; to overfeed it or press it to take something it doesn't want can only be injurious. Whites of egg slip easily down the dog's throat via the loose lips and the natural pouch of the dog's cheek, and dogs can live on this diet alone for some time. Broth made from beef or veal can be jellied and administered easily to the dog. I have found that rabbit's liver will be eaten when everything else has failed to tempt (see "Rabbits as Food"). Brains, and of course milk, are excellent for a sick dog. I saved my dog when she had hard pad by feeding her on a fortified milk substitute given teaspoon by teaspoon. Anything that is concentrated and easily digested can keep the dog's strength up and nourish the body without unduly taxing the digestive organs. If the dog takes something voluntarily, it is worth much more than forcing food down him, and he is less likely to regurgitate it.

One thing that may make my readers smile is my advice not to sympathize with your dog too much when he is ill. If I say to my dog, "Poor Juno! you do look ill," she wilts visibly until she really does look ill. The power of mind over matter counts with dogs as well as with human beings.

To leave the dog to sleep or rest as much as possible is another important part of nursing. Naturally one is so very anxious that one is inclined to return constantly to the dog, hoping for signs of improvement, but these disturbances retard the dog's progress as often as not. Peace and quiet, cleanliness in every matter connected with the patient, warmth with adequate draft-free ventilation, are the general rules for nursing a sick dog.

Skin Diseases. *My dog has developed some bare patches on his back near the tail. They are red, and they cause him to scratch a lot. What can I do to cure this?*

Before discussing the management and treatment of dogs with skin diseases, I feel the reader should know something about the structure of the hair. Practically the whole surface of the body of the dog is covered by hair. Even the stomach, which looks so bare, has very fine hairs, as you will see if you examine it closely. Dogs shed their coats twice a year, but this is the major casting of the coat; actually hair is being shed all the time. This is one reason that dogs should be groomed. There are many different types of hairs; for example, those big thick ones on the lips are called "tactile" hairs, the eyelash hairs are called "cilia," those that are found in the outer ear are termed "tragi," and those in the nostril are "vibrissae." But to the ordinary dog-owner they are all just hairs.

That part of the hair that can be seen above the surface of the skin is known as the "shaft" and that below the skin is the "bulb," capped by the expanded end of the hair root. The sebaceous glands, which produce an oily substance called "sebum," open into the follicles of the hair a little way beneath the surface. It is these little glands that by their copious production make the coat shiny.

When certain skin diseases attack the dog, the parasites enter the hair shaft or follicles and set up intense irritation. Mange is one of the most common of these, and certain varieties are extremely contagious. It is caused by mange mites that look rather like tiny crabs, and the sarcoptes variety, which is the common one in dogs, has suckers on its legs. The treatment of all skin diseases, whether they are infectious or not, must start with a strict diet of health-giving food, with special attention to vitamins to keep the dog's strength up. Infectious mange must be treated professionally, and everything in contact with the dog should be destroyed. But there is one type of mange called "follicular mange" that is common in Dachshunds, Boxers, and Miniature Black-and-Tans, among other breeds, which is not infectious and which is believed to be passed on to the puppies by the mother before birth. At any rate, whether this is true or not, there certainly is a tendency for certain strains in these breeds and other short-coated types of dog to have this disease from a very early age. I once bought a miniature Black-and-Tan that had it at six weeks.

The symptoms are bare patches under the necks and stomachs; the stomachs have little papular spots. Nowadays, although one does not knowingly buy a dog that comes from a strain so afflicted, the cure is easy, namely washing the dog with a pesticidal soap and leaving the soap in. You can get the soap at a drugstore; tell the druggist that you want it for mange.

Eczema, however, is an entirely different type of trouble. It has been proved that its cause is largely dietetic, and several people like Mr. Newman-Turner of Ferne Farm, Shaftesbury, England, have evolved a natural diet that seems to work wonders in these cases. I believe that besides being dietetic in cause, eczema is a nervous disease akin to asthma in humans; if ordinary diet changes fail to cure it, I suggest the proteins in the food be changed until the element to which the dog is allergic is eliminated, after which the condition should clear up. Allergic conditions of this sort have been found to respond magically to antihistamine preparations, which I think proves that dogs, as well as humans, suffer from allergies. Calamine lotion applied to the raw patches relieves the irritation as well. The main thing is to prevent the dog's biting and scratching himself; this is done by enveloping his paws in boots and making him wear a large, flat leather collar called an Elizabeth collar, which prevents him reaching himself on his body to bite it. Most vets have such collars.

It is always better to take expert advice to find out what your dog is suffering from before attempting home treatment, although, as a general rule, fat should certainly be cut out of the diet and greenstuffs added.

Sleeping Arrangements. *I have a medium-sized mongrel; my sister has a Peke. What sort of sleeping quarters would you advise us to provide for them?*

Naturally the answer to this question depends on what sort of living accommodation you occupy. I think all dogs become much nicer dogs when living in close contact with their owners, so in this case I shall assume that the owners are going to keep their dogs in their homes with them. I have dealt in another answer with kennels and their construction.

First of all, I think round baskets for dogs are an abomination. They make the dog sleep in a curled-up position instead of stretched out, which is natural and much more restful for him. Therefore I recommend that the dog's bed be oblong in shape; such beds are readily available.

Alternatively it is a perfectly simple matter to make a bed at home, with three sides of wood and the bottom made either of wood or webbing like a sofa. Bedclothes should consist of padded bedding or the dog's folded blanket. Every dog should have two blankets, which must be laundered fairly frequently to keep the bed clean and sweet-smelling.

Such a bed is suitable for medium-sized terriers and bigger dogs, but I think tiny mites prefer an indoor kennel. If you are rich, you can buy the most beautifully made ones lined with silk; but you can also make one at home out of a wooden box in exactly the same manner as a rabbit hutch. You can house-train the puppy in this kennel because you can make it big enough to have sand at one end, or turf if you can get it, and a blanket at the other. This teaches the dog to be clean. The kennel should be on legs to raise it above drafts and should not be in line with the door. The little toy dog soon learns to go to his own house when he wishes to rest. If you have to leave him alone, the door can be shut and you will know he is safe until your return.

Personally I think the nicest bed for a dog is an old armchair; a wall cupboard or kitchen cupboard with a wire door added also makes an excellent indoor home for a dog. In my opinion, far too much fuss is made about what accommodations a dog needs. A nicely brought up, well-mannered dog fits in anywhere the owner finds for him.

Soft Mouth. *What is the meaning of a "soft mouth" in a dog, and how does one develop it?*

To say that a dog has a soft mouth simply means that the dog is able to carry birds, animals, and other objects in his mouth without damaging them; whereas, if the dog closes its teeth on the thing he is carrying so tightly as to damage it, he has a hard mouth. Some breeds, especially gundogs such as Spaniels and Retrievers, are noted for this soft-mouth characteristic. Poodles also have soft mouths if properly trained, and I find that Great Danes can carry birds and eggs without doing any damage. I have trained my own Great Dane to the gun, and she retrieves birds beautifully.

With most dogs it is a matter of training; any dog that chews what he is carrying must be reprimanded. In obedience training we teach a dog to retrieve a dumbbell and to hold it lightly. Gundog enthusiasts do not believe in using a wooden dumbbell for training Retrievers and use a soft dummy instead, as they believe that using hard objects hardens the dog's tender mouth. I think that it is the training that matters rather than the object. Constant practice bringing things to hand and holding them gently in the mouth until taken from them by the handler is the answer. Should the dog hang on tight to the article, take it from him sharply by jerking it in a downward direction; he will not repeat the offense more than a few times. Any idea that retrieving is a time for playing the fool must be trained out of the dog. The retrieve must be a serious business. It is only when the dog runs off with the article and will not give it up or starts mouthing or tearing it that you run the risk of spoiling his mouth. Never forget either that not all dogs can have a soft mouth, as that depends to a great extent on the conformation of the jaw. A Bulldog would not find it easy to retrieve game; he would almost choke in the attempt.

Unless you intend to use your dog as a gundog, there is not a lot of point in cultivating a soft mouth, but, whether a dog has a soft mouth or not, he should allow his mouth to be handled. A dog that uses his mouth for biting people is to be greatly deplored. Even dogs with soft mouths can bite extremely hard, so never trust any dog that doesn't look too friendly even if it is a so-called soft-mouthed breed.

Teeth. *My puppies' teeth seem to be falling out all over the place. I have no idea when teething takes place; can you enlighten me? Also please tell me something about the care of a dog's teeth.*

Puppies do not have teeth when they are born, but round about the eighteenth day the first ones should pierce the gums. This rate varies according to the breed of dog; some get their teeth out a little later. The first teeth are called milk teeth and number twenty-eight. They are pointed and smaller than the permanent teeth, of which there are normally forty-two but occasionally forty-four in large breeds. By about the fifth week the puppies have a complete set. Owing to the rather softer makeup of these milk teeth, they wear more easily than the permanent ones, and the points of the incisors and tusks are often worn off.

Occasionally the milk teeth are not cast before the permanent ones make their appearance, and it is then necessary to take the offending milk teeth out. Usually, however, if the puppies are given hard biscuits, or large bones that can't splinter their teeth, they will come out by themselves. Dentition is completed at about the fourth month in big breeds and rather later in smaller breeds. Teething time can be a troublesome one, when puppies have been known to get eczema or convulsions. They should be wormed at about four months, as it is often worms rather than teething that cause convulsions. Remember also that milk is essential in the diet of all young dogs. Dogs fed almost entirely on soft foods suffer with tartar much more than dogs that are given something hard to masticate. Scraping the tartar off the dog's teeth is a job for experts and should be done if tartar is present in quantity, as otherwise the gum will be affected and an unhealthy state of the mouth will develop. The dog will get bad breath, and eventually loss of teeth and digestive upsets may follow. The care of the teeth is, in fact, most important. I clean my dogs' teeth with salt on a damp rag, but any tooth powder made for human use will serve also.

Dogs should be trained from an early age to have their mouths examined and handled. Incidentally, it takes an expert to judge the dog's age by its teeth after dentition is complete; as the years pass, the age can be only roughly estimated by the yellow state of the teeth and the presence of tartar.

Telegony. *While she was in heat, my German Shepherd bitch got away, mated with a mongrel, and will shortly have a litter. Does this mean she is now ruined for breeding?*

The old idea that if a bitch escapes and gets mated with a mongrel, she will be forever ruined is rubbish. Telegony, as the transferral of one sire's influence to the offspring of later matings is called, as many followers, but scientifically it is nonsense. What is possible, however, is for a bitch to have pure-bred puppies and mongrels in the same litter, for a bitch will mate several times with different dogs and each mating can produce puppies. That is how this telegony idea has grown up. Naturally a person who has been careless enough to let a valuable bitch out while she is in heat is reluctant to admit it.

Tetanus. *When my dog gets an injury, I am always frightened that he will develop tetanus. What are the symptoms, and how can I guard against it?*

Tetanus or lockjaw is one of the most terrible diseases known, but luckily it is not common in dogs. There are certain tetanus districts where it is wise to get an antitetanus injection for any animal with a puncture or any deep wound. It is those wounds in which oxygen can be assimilated easily that are most likely to get infected. The early symptoms are stiffness and a disinclination to move about, and intolerance to light; later the back legs are held stiffly out behind the dog's body, and his tail is stiff and quivering. Acute digestive disturbances may occur, and gas sometimes collects in the intestines, causing death. The dog does not urinate or pass feces. If he tries to move, he gives an involuntary cry of pain. However, I feel sure that long before these symptoms appear, the owner of a dog would have sought professional advice. The antitetanus toxin is extremely useful in preventing tetanus, but not much use after the infection has got a hold. If your dog ever has a deep wound, the vet will judge whether to give him the antitoxin as a precaution.

Tonsillitis. *My dog doesn't seem to want to eat anything. The little he eats seems to cause him some difficulty in swallowing. What do you think is the matter with him?*

It sounds as if your dog has tonsillitis. Examine the tonsils, which lie on each side of the throat near the back of the tongue. If your dog will let you, gently place your finger or a tongue depressor on the back of the tongue to get a better view. If the tonsils and throat are red, that definitely points to tonsillitis.

As a sore throat can be the start of many diseases, it is wise to take the dog's temperature and consult your vet. First-aid treatment is of course just like that for a human being: a half to a whole aspirin according to size, and keep the patient warm. This is where antibiotics come to the rescue if it is anything more than a mild case. The dog should be given soft foods like ground beef, milk, and a little honey if he will take it.

Travel Sickness. *My dog is sick every time I take her in the car, which makes taking her no pleasure at all. Yet, if she has to stay at home, it restricts our outings. What can I do?*

Dogs are usually sick in cars because they are looking out of the sides of the car rather than the front. They are sick because they are nervous and don't really trust their owners. The only way to get them over this is to train them thoroughly in obedience so that they lie down and stay down quietly in the car; then they will not be sick. I once took a drive with an Irish Setter bitch that had never been driven in a car without being sick in the first few minutes. I sat in the back with her and, in my firmest tone, ordered her to lie down. Incidentally, she was a pupil in my training school and knew that when I gave a command I meant it to be obeyed. She lay down, her head on my lap, and never showed the slightest sign of being sick or even dribbling. This, in my opinion, supports my theory that the owner is to blame for not giving confidence to the dog.

I think it wrong to feed a dog before a journey. Water should be available and reasonable exercise at not too long intervals. I think sedatives extremely useful if a long journey is contemplated, because the owner will be worrying whether the dog is going to be sick, and the dog will pick up the owner's fears and probably will be sick. It might be even more effective if the owner took the sedative!

Always have a puppy's head on your lap when teaching it to be happy in a car. If the puppy is on the floor, the vibrations and the smell from the car will make it sick. As everyone with children knows, fresh air helps to overcome sickness. Dogs, however, should not be allowed to put their heads out of the window for fear of injuring their eyes.

Take your dogs with you everywhere from the time they first come to you and you will have no trouble. I am positive that car sickness is an allergy to cars and the surroundings.

Tumors. *My Great Dane has a swelling on her hock. It seems to me to be growing. What could it be?*

Several of the big breeds of dog are most susceptible to malignant tumors, or cancer, the name by which they are better known. Danes have been known to develop these tumors on the hind leg very quickly for no apparent reason. What happens is that certain cells of the tissues suddenly multiply, eventually eating through the bone. If the malignant tumor does not involve bone substance, as for example in cancer of the mammary tissue, an operation in the early stages can be most effective, but the condition you have noticed in your Dane's hock is quite incurable. The rapid growth of this disease makes it necessary to put the dog to sleep, in spite of the fact that it seems perfectly fit otherwise. If the dog were a toy breed, it might be worthwhile considering the amputation of the affected leg, as tiny dogs are quite capable of running about on three legs. But this cannot be done with a big breed. I lost a very favorite Dane with this complaint.

There are also nonmalignant tumors, which should be removed because of the risk of their turning malignant at a later date.

Consult your vet immediately when you find an unknown swelling, wherever it may be; it may only be a cyst, in which case it can easily be removed. The most common ones found in dogs are the interdigital cysts found between the toes, and the sebaceous cysts that can appear anywhere on the body and that get bigger and bigger until they have a nasty, red, shining surface. These often break, and a blood-stained fluid emerges, as well as a quantity of dried white material—sebum, which has collected instead of being excreted by the glands.

Occasionally bitches suffer from cysts on the ovary, which cause barrenness and suppression of estrus. This condition can be felt by a vet and the cysts broken; the bitch should then return to normal. Bitches in this condition often become extremely bad tempered.

Viciousness. *I have been most gentle with my dog ever since I got him at eight weeks old, yet he snarls at me if I try to take anything from him and even lifts his lip at me if*

I praise him. What can have caused this beloved dog to become so vicious?

If only I could get inside your dog's mind, I have no doubt he would give me a long account of oversoft attentions that he never asked for. I feel certain that he tried as a puppy to do naughty things and you thought that if you spoke gently to him like a child and never lost your temper or raised a finger to him, you were treating him in the kindest and best way possible to ensure that you would have a wonderful companion as he grew up. You must have believed that he would reward you be instant happy obedience. How wrong you were! *Dogs aren't like children; they are like dogs.* They need to be treated like dogs until they have graduated to being like children. You should have trained him firmly and shown him your love unmistakably when he did right. You should have shaken him hard when he threatened to bite you. You should have made him breathless on his choke chain by holding him up on it when he wouldn't drop his bone. He would have had to drop it to avoid choking, and then you should have praised him. It is never too late to learn. Your dog can be made to be a good dog and you a good mistress to him even now. But you will need to alter yourself and your attitude to your dog. You must make him respect you. He even dislikes praise now, because he connects it with something you are asking him to do instead of demanding that he do it. Familiarity breeds contempt. You have been too familiar with your dog before he learned to behave.

Voice. *My dog pays not the slightest attention when I give a command, yet I have seen you training dogs and they watch your face for every order. What is it that I lack?*

You lack a range of tone in your voice sufficient to make your dog interested; you lack surprise in your voice; you lack enthusiasm in your voice. A dog only watches his trainer's

face if he is waiting for every command and for the smile
that eventually leads to the praise and romp he adores. He
also knows when to expect a correction, a firm and unrelenting one, if he does wrong. I mean to win. You obviously
don't mind that much. I feel terribly proud when my pupils
do well. I could almost eat them, I love them so much. My
tone ranges from a high squeak of joy to a low tone of "I
mean it." I clap when a dog does right—I have to, I feel so
happy. Do you ever let yourself go to this extent? I doubt
it. Give it a try.

Worms, Parasitic. *Please tell me what to look for in my dog
to find out if it is infected with worms?*

There are numerous kinds of worms that infect dogs—
intestinal, blood, stomach, among others—but the most
common are the round worms and tapeworms. Worms in
puppies cause endless trouble and can be seen when passed
as round white things pointed at both ends. Puppies with
worms are often potbellied and, if you look at the tummy,
it often has a bluish tinge. The coat is poor and the puppy
often doesn't thrive. Contrarily I have seen puppies thrive
very well who have, when wormed, passed large quantities
of round worms. Dogs afflicted with worms often have a
terrific appetite, but the food does them no good. There are
a mass of worm cures on the market. I would recommend a
beginner to send the puppy to the vet to be properly
wormed, as vets have stronger cures. Puppies should be
wormed at twelve weeks and six months and then once
more if any signs of worms persist.

People tend to ask: "Where can my dog have picked up
worms?" The answer is: eating grass, drinking from pools,
eating dung, and many other causes. Round worms are not
communicable to man, but tapeworm is, and it can cause a
very serious disease of the muscles in man; so if any flat
segments of worm are ever seen in the stool, the dog should

be immediately treated for tapeworms. On no account whatsoever let the dog eat off plates or dishes used by human beings; do not kiss the dog, or let your face anywhere near his muzzle, as he licks his rear portions and the eggs may be carried on the muzzle. These worms can cause paralysis in the dog. Rabbits are the intermediate hosts of tapeworms, so it is dangerous to give raw rabbit, in my opinion. The dog should be treated professionally.

Some puppies get worms through the bloodstream of their dams: that is the reason a bitch should be wormed in the early stages of pregnancy or before mating. Cleanliness in everything to do with dogs is essential.

X Rays. *My dog has swallowed a safety pin. He doesn't seem any the worse for it. Can he be X-rayed to find out where it is?*

You would be surprised how many vets these days use X rays in their practices. If your vet hasn't got a machine, he will soon put you in touch with a vet who has. Veterinary colleges and animal medical centers certainly have X-ray facilities.

X rays are extremely useful in diagnosis, and safe in experienced hands. No dog should be X-rayed often as it may damage the bone marrow, producing leukemia; that is why the medical profession keeps telling people not to use shoe X rays often.

X rays are invaluable in diagnosing fractures. They can be used to diagnose tumors, as well as foreign bodies. You tell me your dog has swallowed a safety pin; when he is X-rayed, you may find that much more than that has been swallowed. Occasionally it is necessary to give some sort of anesthetic to a dog that has to be X-rayed, as he will not otherwise stay absolutely still.

Stones in the kidney can be seen by X rays, and many other troubles, like stricture of the stomach, for the diagnosis of which a barium meal is used as with human beings.

Even pregnancy in valuable bitches has been diagnosed early in this way, but there again it is not advisable to use X rays unless absolutely necessary for the reason given above.

Yellows. *My neighbor says her dog is suffering from "the yellows." What does she mean?*

This is another word for jaundice and is dealt with under that heading.

Zymotic Disease. *Somebody trying to show off the other day bet me I didn't know what zymotic disease was. He insisted it occurred in dogs. I can't find it in any book I have. Please enlighten me.*

I think your friend must have been doing a crossword puzzle because this word is hardly ever used nowadays. It was formerly used for diseases like distemper, which owe their origin to some morbific principle (rather like fermentation) in the system. The word and its explanation are out of date.

The
A to Z
of Puppies

A TO Z OF PUPPIES

Age. *What is the best age to buy a puppy?*

The best age at which to buy a puppy is approximately six to eight weeks, when it has been safely weaned and is no longer in need of the warmth of its brothers and sisters. Many people buy them younger; I knew one that I am sure was no older than one month when it was bought, but the rearing of such a puppy is hazardous. Much depends on the size of the puppy you choose. If you are determined to buy the runt of the litter, then it may be wise to wait a week longer before having it than if you were buying the pick of the litter.

Dogs very often develop earlier than bitches, but don't be deceived by their little extra size—they are not always the strongest. Puppies should be completely weaned from the mother by six weeks. If you have a warm place for it and sensible ideas about its feeding and rest, if you do not allow young children to maul it and do not expect too rapid house-training (for puppies of that age have no control over their bladders or bowels at all), then by all means buy one that is six weeks old. Many breeders, not wishing for unpleasantness if anything goes wrong, will not part with puppies of this age.

It is quite impossible to know what six-week-old puppies

are going to look like at four months. Their eyes are all the same dark blue, when in two months' time they may be a pale yellow, which is unattractive in most dogs. So if you mind this sort of thing, don't buy one that's too young. Color changes must be reckoned on as well, for at six weeks the puppy only has his baby coat, and this will not be shed for some time. When his permanent coat does come through, the color and texture will be somewhat different. Of course, brindles don't become fawns or vice versa, because color is hereditary, and one can know roughly before buying a puppy what it is likely to look like when adult. For example, in Great Danes two fawns mated together can produce only fawns; a brindle + fawn mating will produce brindles and fawns. Color study is most interesting but beyond the scope of this book.

Allergy. *My puppy has lots of tiny red spots on his tummy and seems forever scratching; the vet says he thinks it is an allergy to something. What does he mean?*

An allergy means a sensitivity to something or other; usually a food of some kind. Heat bumps in children are an example. Perhaps your puppy has an allergy to eggs, or fish, or even milk with the cream on it. Perhaps you have bathed it in some kind of medicated shampoo to which its skin is sensitive. Only by a process of elimination will you be able to find out what is causing this irritation. In the meantime, just to make sure the vet is right in his diagnosis, I strongly advise you to bathe the dog in a good pesticidal soap that the druggist can recommend for mange; when you have washed the puppy, dry it with the soap left in. This will make sure the spots you mention are not follicular mange, which has the same symptoms and which the soap will cure.

To stop the puppy from scratching so much, if it is an allergy, dab the spots with witch hazel or double-strength calamine lotion. Do not apply the lotion too thickly as it has slightly poisonous tendencies if licked off in quantity, though this is most unlikely to occur.

Occasionally, when a puppy is teething, it gets a teething rash in the same way a baby does. If this is so, fuller's earth powdered on the irritating spots will have a soothing effect and is quite harmless.

Anemia. *The vet says my puppy is anemic. Please explain what he means.*

Anemia is caused by fewer and smaller red cells in the blood, which make the bloodstream lack hemoglobin. It is seen in the pale appearance of the gums, tongue, and mucous membrane of the eyes. The cure is to give iron in the form of ferrous sulfate tablets, one to three per day according to the size of the puppy. You cannot harm the puppy by giving too many. Iron does sometimes cause constipation, however, so watch its bowel movements and, if necessary, give a teaspoonful of medicinal paraffin per day until corrected. When a dog is taking iron, its stool will be black.

Appetite. *My puppy never seems hungry. What should I do?*

A puppy's appetite should always be keen. The puppy who doesn't bolt its food is not completely healthy. You are either overfeeding or wrongly feeding it.

The number of meals a puppy needs must, of course, be governed by its age and size, but at six weeks old it should have five or six small meals a day. (I go into diet under the section "Feeding.") A lot of people overfeed their puppies just because they appear hungry. A rough estimate of the needs in food of a puppy is one-half ounce of food per pound body weight, but this can be wrong for the larger breeds. The rate of growth is so fast that the puppy would be grossly overfed if you stuck to this at about four months. If the appetite is poor, cut the quantity of food until the appetite returns, having made sure the puppy is well. Frequent small feedings are better than less frequent large ones.

Fat is a thing small puppies seem unable to digest in great quantities, and this often gives a puppy a poor appetite. Cut out eggs, use skimmed milk, and give lean scraped beef, and the puppy's appetite should then return. Sometimes the puppy has a depraved appetite. It will wolf manure, stones, and filth of any kind as if it were starving, yet leave good food. This is usually a sign of mineral deficiency. I know of some kennels that allow their dogs to eat horse dung because it is so rich in minerals. I won't recommend this as a thing to do, when a vitamin-and-mineral supplement like Squibbs's Vionate can provide all that is necessary in a puppy's diet. I know vitamins and minerals are expensive, but the forming of a puppy's bones and teeth will reflect on the dog's health for the rest of his life.

A puppy should lick its dish feverishly when it has had its meal; that shows it would eat more and its appetite is good. Don't be tempted to give it more than the right amount or its digestion will suffer. A puppy's tummy is very tiny, and if you distend it with too big a meal, the puppy will get flatulent; a big puppy may get so heavy from overfeeding that its front legs bow.

A puppy should always be ready for its meals. If it isn't, don't leave the food about; take it and throw it away, for the food should always be completely fresh. If the puppy doesn't want its food for more than one meal, consult your vet; it is probably sickening for something.

Aptitude. *My puppy seems unbelievably stupid. Are some dogs born cleverer than others?*

In the matter of intelligence, dogs, like human beings, vary enormously. The development of the brain is to a certain extent hereditary. The puppy must have an aptitude for the work it is expected to carry out. For example, Pekes wouldn't make good gundogs; their physical form doesn't lend itself to this work. Some breeds undoubtedly, through generations of training for work, have developed better brain power than others. The German Shepherd, Poodle, and Labrador all show a quick alertness that makes training them easy. On the other hand, Dalmatians are not so easily educated.

If the aptitude is there, it is up to the owners to encourage the dog to use its brains, and if training goes steadily along set lines, this development of brain power is quite remarkable. Few owners really get the best out of their dogs: they should start developing the puppy's aptitude for work at a very early age. In fact, I think eight weeks old is the time to begin in a small way. The puppy should be talked to in a sensible way; made to do things for you like carrying things; taught words like "Here's master, go and see him"; "Who's that?" "See them off!" and other sentences that are relevant to everyday life in the home. I think the aptitude of the owner for training the puppy is more essential than the aptitude of the puppy to absorb the training.

Arrival of the Puppy. *I am expecting a six-week-old Dachshund puppy to arrive by rail next week. What preparations should I make for its welcome?*

The first thing to do is to make sure that the sender of the puppy notifies you in ample time what train it is on and the time of its arrival so that you can be at the station to meet it, especially if it is coming a long distance. We hope the box it is sent in will be a warm and comfortable one, large enough to allow the puppy to move around in, yet not so big that it catches cold. A six-week-old puppy is rather too young, in my opinion, to travel far, for it needs warmth, and feeding five times a day.

You must find out from the person it is coming from exactly what it has been fed on, and at what mealtimes it has each kind of food. Some diet charts that are sent out by breeders look unnecessarily complicated and expensive, and one often wonders whether the puppy really has had such food. But since it is very unwise to change the feeding of a young puppy, go by the chart for at least a week, and then, if you wish, modify it in slow stages.

You must decide beforehand exactly where you intend keeping the puppy. It is not enough to say that the kitchen, for example, will do; you must also have made preparations to house it so that it can be kept very warm at first. The only way to do this is to have an indoor kennel. This need not be an elaborate affair, but it should be made large enough so that the puppy can still use it as his rest place when he grows old enough to be free in the house. There is nothing so useful as to have somewhere you can put the dog, knowing it cannot get into mischief when you are out or busy for a few hours. You will find full particulars under "Kennels" on how to make an indoor kennel; if you haven't the skill or facilities for making one, you can buy one readymade.

The most important thing to arrange before a puppy joins the household is to think how it is going to fit in with the daily life and routine of the home. So many people just buy a puppy on impulse, never realizing that a young puppy is almost as much trouble to begin with as a baby if you wish to train it quickly to be a trouble-free occupant of the home. People forget that if you want, for example, to house-train a puppy quickly, you cannot, at first, go out to dinner and the theater, for the hours you would be away would mean that you could not take the puppy out often enough to make it clean. When I had a new puppy recently, I gave up six weeks of my life to its early training and reckoned the time well spent. Few people, I think, would take their duty to their puppy as seriously as that.

Providing the food the puppy requires includes added extra minerals and vitamins. These are most important in the larger breeds and the cost is quite considerable, but the forming of the bone structure is vital in the early days and must never be sacrificed. (See "Minerals.")

From the very beginning it must be decided which member of the household is going to look after the puppy, and as far as possible the routine should be stuck to. Puppies get set in their ways, and a strict routine is essential for health and training.

Having bought the food the puppy is accustomed to, having made an indoor kennel as a reception center for it, and, if possible, having taken up any very valuable carpet in case of house-training mistakes, the new owner is ready for its arrival. There are on the market two preparations that help with house-training. One is a "puppy trainer," of which two drops on a newspaper encourage the puppy to "puddle" on that spot, and the other is a preparation to stop urine from taking the color out of a carpet. Both of these are most useful with a new puppy. Read as much as you can about care of dogs and all should go well.

Barking. *My five-month-old puppy makes no attempt to bark at strangers who come to the door. When should it start this?*

There can be no hard and fast rule about barking. A lot depends on whether the puppy is the only one in the house or whether there is an older dog who will teach it what to do. If it is an only dog, then the owner must teach it to bark by running to the door and saying "Who is it?" in a very fierce and excited voice, and if necessary barking himself.

To teach a dog to bark on command is also a very difficult thing to do. As a trick it is very effective. It can only be taught by bribery and "woofing" yourself when knocking on the door or table, and giving the command "Speak." If the puppy is hungry enough it will learn that the slightest bark gets food, and will quickly cotton on to what is wanted of it. For some time, give a tidbit as a reward. This can be stopped when the action becomes almost automatic. In my opinion, all puppies need bribery.

Barking can become a menace and must be stopped when

the owner gives the command "Cease." If the puppy doesn't stop at once, it must be made to lie down and stay down, when it cannot so easily bark.

Dogs can become such terrible barkers that they have to be put to sleep because they are a nuisance to the neighbors. A small operation cutting the vocal cords can stop a dog's barking and, as far as I know, it is painless and doesn't make a dog a bit unhappy. It is, of course, a last resort and should never be done to a trainable puppy.

Baskets. *I am expecting a new Labrador puppy to arrive here next week. It is ten weeks old. What sort of basket should I get for it?*

A basket for a ten-week-old puppy is not a good idea. Puppies need rest. If allowed to follow the owners about in the house, it will get overtired. A ten-week-old puppy should have an indoor kennel like a rabbit hutch made for it, with its bedding at one end and newspaper at the other, so that if a mistake is made, it doesn't matter. When the dog is about six months old, it can have a basket, but personally I don't like round ones. The puppy's natural sleeping position, when really sound asleep, is on its side with its legs stretched out. Unless the basket is much too big for it, this attitude cannot be achieved. Therefore I think an oblong bed on legs is a much better sleeping arrangement for the puppy. Best of all, I like an old chair, which has the advantage of being off the floor, with side protection to keep the puppy free from drafts. The puppy must be taught from an early age to go to its bed and stay there when told. If visitors come to the house, the puppy is then not a nuisance to them.

Baths. *Should I bathe my puppy? He smells.*

You do not say how old your puppy is, but if he is about eight to twelve weeks old and has lice or smells bad, then it may be necessary to bathe him. There is nothing injurious in the bathing process. The trouble lies in getting the puppy absolutely dry afterward. Nowadays many people have home hair driers. There is nothing better than a hair drier for drying a puppy. It not only dries him but gets him used to something new, which is always good. Be sure to keep your own hand underneath him all the time to make sure he is not getting too hot. The drier must not be held too near the pup's tender skin. A good rub with a rough towel to get the worst of the water off before useing the hair drier is always necessary.

Use a good pesticidal dog soap. The soap can be dried in for extra protection against reinfestation. Such soap also cures follicular mange, commonly found in Dachshunds, Boxers, and similar short-coated breeds.

Bedding. *What sort of bedding should I put in my puppy's kennel? She lives outside.*

There are lots of different kinds of bedding—hay, straw, wood shavings. One can also buy manufactured types of bedding. The main thing to remember is that a small puppy must not be wet; so whatever bedding you use, it must be frequently examined and changed if wet or dirty. Dirty bedding makes a dirty puppy. It is useless to put blankets for a small puppy in its outside kennel. But newspaper or blankets make quite a good bed for a small puppy kept warm indoors. Until the puppy is house-trained, newspaper is the most easily disposed of. Whatever bedding you use, if the kennel is not made draft-proof and watertight, the puppy will catch a chill. The construction of the kennel is of more importance than the type of bedding.

Bee Stings. *My puppy got stung by a bee, and her face got very swollen. What should I have done?*

Bicarbonate of soda is what you should apply to a bee

sting. Sometimes bee stings can cause tremendous allergic reaction. If the vet is not available and you have any antihistamine capsules in the house for hay fever, give the puppy half or one according to age—over five months, one capsule. These will make the puppy sleepy but will help to stop further swelling. Ice, too, acts to control swelling.

It is an emergency if a puppy gets stung on the tongue, as it could choke. Any druggist would give you an antihistamine pill in this emergency, I am sure, even if it is a prescription drug. Your vet should be called as soon as possible.

Beef. *What is the best kind of beef to feed my puppy?*

I think the upper shin is best. It is not so sinewy as the leg of beef itself and can be easily scraped with a sharp knife for a small puppy. The outside can be boiled down for gravy. Neck of beef comes second, to my way of thinking. Naturally I am not considering the expensive cuts. Raw beef is always better for a young puppy than cooked, although as the puppy gets older, it must get accustomed to digesting cooked meat; but raw meat is more easily digested at first.

For an older puppy one can buy ground beef quite cheaply, but this always contains more fat and is not so good for a young puppy. Never feed pork to a puppy. Mutton and veal can be fed if you wish.

Biting. *My eight-week-old puppy bites me unmercifully. Will he grow out of this? His teeth are like needles.*

Never allow puppies to bite hard enough to hurt you. All puppies use their teeth in play and when angry, and only you can tell which sort of bite it is. But whichever it is, when the bite becomes hard enough to hurt, the puppy must be corrected firmly with such words as, "No bite." If it doesn't stop, shake it by catching hold of the loose skin of its neck on both sides under the ears, and make it look you straight in the face. If you sound angry enough, the puppy will quickly understand. If you permit it to bite one time and then get annoyed the next, the puppy will be bewildered. Be consistent in all you do with your puppy.

Blebs. *My Golden Retriever puppy, which is ten months old, has abscesses that suppurate between his toes. He licks them furiously all day and they burst. What do you think I should do for them?*

These swellings between the toes are commonly known as "blebs." They are caused by a staphylococcus infection, or they can come from a thorn prick. Dogs in poor condition are particularly susceptible to them. Some vets operate on them and remove them, but they usually come again.

An "autogenous" vaccine made by taking some of the infected fluid from the blebs and having a vaccine made from it has been found to be effective in some cases, but I have found in practice that blebs are highly sensitive to aureomycin. Aureomycin, in pills or capsules as prescribed by a vet, or applied to the blebs in the form of an ointment, completely clears up this annoying and painful condition.

It is essential to keep the puppy from licking these blebs, which will retard healing. Therefore you must make socks for him. Proper boots can now be bought at high-class dog shops in London and in America, so that if you place an old cotton sock on first, and then the boot, the dog cannot bite the blebs. If the dog tears the boot off, he must be muzzled. It is essential for them to heal naturally—a thing they cannot do if licked by the puppy.

Bleeding. *My puppy cut her paw on a broken milk bottle. She bled an awful lot. What should I have done to stop it?*

I think it unlikely that the wound you describe was a severed artery. Your dog would die very quickly if you couldn't stop the bleeding from an artery. I think the wound was "veinous." You can always tell which it is by the color of the blood and whether it is pumping or not. If it is bright in color and pumping, the puppy has cut an artery. If the flow is regular and darker in color, a vein has been cut.

If the puppy has severed an artery, you must apply a tourniquet at once by using your handkerchief or a piece of rag. Tie a knot on the side of the limb nearest to the heart, place a twig or pencil in the knot, and twist until the bleeding stops. Do not tie it so tight that you cause an injury to the limb. Loosen the tourniquet every ten minutes to see if the bleeding has stopped. Take the puppy to the vet as quickly as you can. If the cut is just an ordinary one, apply pressure to the wound itself and hold it there for at least two minutes. After two minutes of "bleeding time," the blood should coagulate and the bleeding stop. Most cuts due to glass need a stitch or two, and if they are deep enough to need stitching, they are deep enough to warrant an antitetanus injection. With deep wounds there is an ever-present risk of tetanus infection.

Body Temperature. *What is a normal puppy's temperature?*

The normal temperature of a puppy is 101.5-102°F. If the weather is very hot or the puppy has been dashing around a lot, 0.5° higher wouldn't be much to worry about. Anything over 102° should be treated with suspicion.

Heavy panting is a sign of rising temperature, unless the puppy has been playing violently. In the hot summer it should not play too much in the sun. Puppies sweat through the tongue and nose. The do not have sweat glands in the body. Too much heat can cause a heatstroke. This must be treated by putting the puppy in a cool place. In a real emergency the puppy may have to be immersed in cool water to bring the temperature down to 103°, which is reasonably safe. It must, of course, be thoroughly dried or it will catch a chill. Cool water should be available for drinking. If a puppy is ever off color, take its temperature; if it is normal, there is nothing serious. The temperature of a puppy rises and falls very quickly.

Bones. *Everyone tells me something different about giving bones to puppies. What is your opinion on this matter?*

Every puppy needs something to gnaw to help him over the teething period. But be careful to give him only big raw marrow bones, with the marrow itself scooped out. The reason for this is that marrow is very fatty, and few puppies tolerate fat well. I always cut off any large lumps of fat still adhering to the bone and any loose cartilage. Some people pressure-cook the bones after the puppy has finished gnawing them, and with this method the bones are reduced to powder. This powder is good in small quantities, being full of calcium and other minerals, but it does make the puppy very constipated and makes its stool hard and grainy. Game, chicken, and mutton bones, which splinter, are not safe for puppies. Be sure that when your butcher saws the shin bone in half, he does so without splintering it, as small splinters could fatally injure your puppy's intestines. A new bone every few days keeps a puppy occupied for hours. The only thing to be careful of is inflammation of the eyes, which can happen to a puppy that gnaws and gnaws. The bottom lids swell up, fall away a bit from the eye, and are very inflamed. I think the cause must be the pressure on the upper jawbone. Optrex or aureomycin eye ointment has a soothing effect on this condition.

Once a puppy is adult, an occasional shinbone helps to keep the teeth white and free from tartar, which, if not scaled from the teeth at regular intervals, produces receding gums and pyorrhea.

Stock from the simmering of all bones is extremely good if it is poured over the afternoon feed of bread or biscuit.

But always let it cool first so that the fat can be skimmed off. Odd scraps of leftover vegetables can be added to this stock, as they are rich in vitamins.

Bottle Feeding. *I am trying to rear a litter of puppies on the bottle—the mother has no milk. How should I do it?*

The best thing to do is to leave the puppies with their mother for warmth and toilet attention, and in the hope that she may be giving them a little natural milk, and to supplement the feeds with Enfamil or Similac. If the puppies are newly born, a doll's bottle is the best thing to use—the tiny nipples are just right for small puppies, but for big breeds, use a nipple like the ones designed for rearing baby lambs. Newborn puppies must be fed every two hours during the night as well as during the day. Slowly let the intervals lengthen out until at three weeks old they are fed every four hours during the day and only once during the night. At three weeks old they can have scraped beef. Some puppies will eat a little scraped beef as early as fourteen days old. The most important thing is to get them taking supplementary food as soon as possible.

Naturally the easiest thing to do with orphan puppies is to get a foster mother so that the artificial feeding is only a temporary measure. Veterinarians may know of lactating bitches who can take on foster pups. Local newspapers and radio stations have helped desperate owners to find foster mothers—even TV newscasters have been known to put out an SOS.

It is impossible in this book to specify the quantity of milk food to give each puppy; this depends on the size and breed. See what the puppy will take; it is the best judge.

Bowels. *How often should my puppy empty its bowels?*

This is a difficult question to answer. It all depends on what you feed it and how often it has its meals. A tiny puppy usually empties its bowels four or five times a day, but as it gets older, once or twice a day is usual. It is most important to teach a puppy regularity. Take it to the same spot each time, giving some consistent command like "Hurry up"; when it performs, praise it enthusiastically. If you train a puppy from the moment it comes into your home, you will be able to take it confidently to other people's houses, knowing it has performed its functions and is unlikely to offend at your friend's house. People do not like dogs to soil their gardens, let alone their houses.

Remember, children may play near where you have let your dog empty its bowels. Try and choose a place where people are unlikely to walk in it, and *never* allow it to soil the pavement—it is always possible to push the puppy to the curb.

The consistency of the puppy's stool should be mainly firm, but not too hard or it may hurt the puppy to pass it. A milky diet has the effect of making a puppy's stool loose. Any signs of diarrhea must be dealt with at once by consulting your vet. Many illnesses start with diarrhea. In the case of looseness, give, according to the size of the puppy, a teaspoonful to a tablespoonful of Kaopectate every four hours or until a vet can be consulted. This mixture can be got at any druggist and is a good first-aid remedy.

Bread. *Which do you think it best to feed a puppy on— bread or dog biscuits?*

I don't think there is such a word as "best" in connection with the feeding of a puppy. There are excellent puppy meals and biscuits on which the puppy will thrive just as well as on bread. On the other hand, wholemeal bread takes a lot to beat it in its natural form.

White bread must never be fed to puppies as it is made from agenized flour and is said to cause hysteria in dogs. Stale bread is better than new bread, and oven-toasted bread is best of all. The bread can be fed with a little butter on it or soaked in milk or gravy. It is bread or biscuits that give bulk to the puppy's meals, and it should be part of every puppy's diet.

When a puppy is very tiny, many people feed it on farina instead of bread or biscuits. I have always found Cornflakes to be unsurpassed as breakfast for a Great Dane puppy. A big dog needs the nourishment without the bulk, and Cornflakes provide just that.

Remember, if you feed a puppy on biscuits or puppy meal, these must be soaked in boiling water first. Never give meal dry; it will swell inside the puppy's tummy and distend it, and may make the puppy ill.

Four slices of brown bread is what I have found adequate for the evening meal of most medium-sized dogs. One thinnish slice is enough for a small dog.

Breed Clubs. *I am very interested in showing my Basenji. What advantages would I gain by joining a breed club?*

The advantages you get from joining a club devoted to your breed are usually reduced entry fees to their shows, probably a monthly news sheet, and the chance to mix with people who are the experts in your breed and who are only too anxious to further the success of the breed.

Breeds usually have more than one club, and breeds with large registrations may have several clubs. Most breed clubs offer a variety of trophies at shows, and the winners hold the trophy for a year, or for an otherwise specified time. The breed club also guarantees entry fees for shows, which helps secretaries to put on classes for the particular breed.

The American Kennel Club will give you names and addresses of its member breed clubs.

Brushing. *What kind of brush should I get for my Poodle puppy?*

The best type of brush for any long-haired dog is a

wire-bristled brush. Nylon is not as good. Always brush in the direction in which the hair grows. The puppy should learn to lie on its side to be brushed. Always brush from its tummy left to right, and brush the hair toward you. After this, if you have brushed it properly, you can comb it without pulling any hair out. Turn the puppy on the other side and do the same thing. Should there be any matting of the coat, gently pull the mat apart with your finger and thumb, and then comb it through. Lastly, stand the puppy up and brush its topside. Always be sure to get the brush right down to the skin. Be very careful when brushing the head not to hurt the puppy's eyes. To brush the ears, hold them in your hands and brush downward and then upward before combing.

Short-haired dogs should be groomed with a hound brush, which is worn over the owner's hand with the end of the thumb outside. This has the grooming part over the palm of the hand, and the puppy usually loves the massaging that this type of grooming gives him. Finish off the grooming with an old piece of silk to give a lovely bloom to the coat.

Burns. *My puppy burned itself against the fire. What is the first-aid remedy for this?*

All burns should have a paste of bicarbonate of soda and water. Spread it well over the affected parts. It soon relieves the pain.

Guards should be on all fires in a house where a puppy lives. They don't seem to have any natural fear of fire these days. I think the old natural instincts in dogs are fading out. The safest type of guard is one with a top to it since a big puppy can stand on the fender and drop something into the fire quite easily. I had that happen with my own Dane. Now my fireplace is completely shut in with a guard.

If you haven't any bicarbonate of soda in the house at the moment the burn occurs, an anesthetic ointment like

Nupracanol is the next best thing. Cover the burn up, if possible with a pad of the ointment.

Cabbage and Greens. *Shall I give my puppy vegetables?*

If your puppy likes vegetables, there is no reason to deny them to him in small quantities, but there is no necessity to give vegetables. A dog is a carnivorous animal. I know there are vitamins in vegetables that are, of course, good for puppies, but I presume you are adding vitamins to the dog's diet anyway, so that this form is unnecessary. Just because puppies eat grass doesn't mean they need vegetables; grass-eating is done to assist evacuation of the bowels. There are several kinds of grass dogs eat; some make them sick, others act as an aperient. Herb Royal Ltd., 40 St. Mary Street, Bridgwater, England, supplies herbal products making grass unnecessary for town-dwellers' dogs. Similar products are available in the United States.

My own puppy adores apples, so I give her pieces of apple as a reward for doing something clever. This is much better than giving chocolate or sweets.

Cancer. *I had to put my last dog to sleep at only six years old because of cancer. How can I protect my new puppy from this?*

I only wish I knew the answer to this problem. In dogs the cancer is a sarcoma. For some extraordinary reason the cells start multiplying in a bone area, and the bone eventually breaks. There is no known cure.

The cancer often begins after a blow. As far as possible, prevent your puppy from getting bone injuries. It is most unlikely that cancer will ever appear in a puppy; it is a disease of the aging dog. Usually the cancer not only affects the bone but in time spreads to other parts of the body. So, if cancer is evident, you must face up to the fact that you will not have your dog with you long, and another puppy should be brought to live with you and make the loss less painful.

Occasionally a longer life has been given to a favorite dog by removing the affected bone, but this is not possible in big dogs. I knew a Terrier that ran about for years with only three legs. It appeared perfectly happy.

Canker. *My dog scratches his ears a lot. What is wrong?*

He probably has canker, which is due to a brownish discharge that comes from inflammation of the lining of the external part of the ear. It is usually started by an excessive amount of wax, which leads to superficial inflammation and infection by germs. Sometimes it is caused by lice, but more often by the parasite that causes auricular mange, which gives intense irritation.

This discharge from canker is very horrid, and can get mixed up with the hair of dogs such as Cocker Spaniels and cause them to smell very badly.

In mild cases the outer ear can be gently cleaned with 10% volume hydrogen peroxide and warm water, and a few drops of the peroxide can be dropped into the inner ear.

Unless you are experienced with dogs, it can be dangerous to probe into the inner ear to cleanse it. It is best to take the dog to a vet. Nowadays antibiotics are used to kill infection and alleviate the inflammation.

Canker and eczema often get mixed up. Canker is a name given to a multitude of troubles in the ear. There is actually no disease called canker; it is just a group of maladies, each with its own individual name. But for the ordinary owner the word canker sums up trouble with the ear.

Eczema, however, is usually a dietetic disease. It can cause intense irritation, and the puppy scratches the hair off the ears, leaving bleeding patches. In all cases the diet should be changed so that less meat and a more farinaceous diet with plenty of milk is given. Herb Royal Products of

Bridgwater, Somerset, England, have a herbalistic diet, which they swear by.

The raw surfaces can be dabbed with calamine lotion. A tonic full of minerals and vitamins is also a good idea; if the puppy is given Vionate from its early days, eczema seldom gets a hold.

Some people have found that antihistamine drugs such as are used for hay fever in humans have very often a remarkable effect. This may show that eczema comes from giving the wrong kind of protein or too much protein in the diet. A good eczema ointment can be effective inside the ear, but ointments are messy outside.

Any serious trouble with a puppy's ears should be reported to your vet, as deafness can result, and there is nothing so miserable as owning a deaf dog.

Cars. *My puppy jumps all over the car when I'm driving. How can I teach it to stay quiet?*

If you want a puppy to be really intelligent, you must, as far as possible, take it with you wherever you go. Rides in the car should be a pleasure not a curse. People with station wagons have no trouble at all. They can just put a wire-netting frame in between the puppy and the passenger seat; then the puppy cannot annoy anyone. But if the puppy is to be a pleasure to take with you, it must stay put in the back seat of the car. This can be achieved by tying a rope between the two window handles to which you attach a piece of chain or cord on a loop to the puppy's collar. It will thus be able to move about but not get off the seat. By far the best thing is to teach it to "sit" and "stay," or "down" and "stay," in the back. It cannot, however, be taught this when you are on your own; you need a helper, because at first the dog will get up again and again. Only by being firm and, as often as it gets up, pushing it down with a very firm command "down" can you hope to teach it. This cannot be done while you are at the wheel.

If the puppy is not too big, it can, of course, have a kennel made like a rabbit hutch put on the back seat and travel in that. Thus the puppy can see out but not get out. It will soon get used to being there alone and later it can be free.

Everything to do with puppies is learned by force of habit. Once you have accustomed a puppy to doing something at a certain time or in a certain manner, it will do that in the future without fuss.

Car Sickness. *My puppy slobbers all over when I take her in the car. What can I do to stop it?*

This car sickness is caused by the puppy's not trusting you. By taking her everywhere with you in your car from her earliest days, she will quickly get used to the car's motion. She should always lie on someone's lap to begin with and not on the car floor. Tie a bib around her neck if necessary, and give no food before a journey. With obedience training, car sickness disappears. It is only high-strung puppies who suffer from this trouble. Placid puppies aren't car-sick. Of course, if the owner is perpetually worrying about the puppy, it will make the animal sick. Put some old blanket in the car, and don't worry. Provided the puppy has not been fed, it will only dribble saliva, which easily sponges off.

Castration. *My puppy, although only eight months old, is intensely "sexy." He is a nuisance with every dog he meets. What can I do?*

Castration is the best way to deal with an oversexed puppy. He will not get better as he grows older, as some people would have you believe; he will get worse. Destructive acts such as tearing up bedding are all part of the sex urge, and eventually he will mount people's legs to the intense embarrassment of those concerned. Castration, if done young, has no bad effect on the puppy at all, and the result will be fairly speedy. If left until the dog is really a confirmed nuisance, it takes much longer to have effect. Most vets do the operation overnight and let the puppy go home next morning. There need be no stitches in the incision. After a week the puppy is quite over it. Some vets put in stitches, but these do occasionally get infected. So keep an eye on the puppy's backside for at least a week to see that all is healing well.

A castrated puppy should be strictly dieted to keep his figure. He is inclined to beg for food. There are no harmful effects after castration. I think all male dogs kept as pets would only benefit by this operation. They are much nicer to own, and remain gay and happy.

Cats. *How can I make my cat friends with my new puppy?*

This is a very knotty problem and one that often has no solution. If your cat has ever been friendly with a dog, there should not be much to worry about. Just keep the puppy from annoying the cat for about a week; but if the cat has never seen a dog before, it will take much longer. I take the cat and dog onto my lap and stroke them both hard, not allowing the cat to run away. The other method I have used is to make a double cage divided by strong wire netting and make them sleep side by side. After this there is seldom any more trouble. Some cats, however, are born nasty with dogs, and it will not be safe for any puppy to be with that type of cat, for it will surely scratch the puppy's eyes.

Never encourage any puppy to chase cats; it is cruel and quite useless—the dog will never catch the cat, even if that is why you teach it to be so horrid. Should it show any signs of cat-chasing, put it on a long cord if a cat is likely to be around and when it starts to go after the cat, jerk really hard on the check cord, and give the puppy a tremendous scolding with the word "leave." Cat-chasing may easily lead to chicken-chasing or even sheep-killing. It is up to you to check this tendency from the start. A small kitten and a puppy are ideal friends, and there is no better way to teach friendliness than to have one of each. Don't be worried if the puppy occasionally carries the cat around by the neck. This frequently happens and is only a sign of good friendship.

Character. *When breeding puppies, can you stamp character of a certain kind by always using the same strain of stud dog and brood bitch?*

In theory one can do a lot more with breeding than one can do in practice. The study of genetics is fascinating but hardly suitable for this little book. By linebreeding one can fix certain characteristics, but the puppies are often a disappointment when one has tried so hard to breed perfection.

I think that breeding for character is far more important than anything else. I am horrified with the way breeders, without conscience, pass on character and temperament faults they know to be present in the parents. Nerves are a hereditary factor; they come out generation after generation, as bad temper does also. Therefore, see the parents of any puppy you buy, if this is humanly possible. Your whole existence can be wrecked by owning a fierce dog or a very nervous one.

Certain colors are more dominant than others, and you can be certain of what color you are going to breed. If you want to breed puppies yourself, you need a book that deals in detail with genetics.

Chickens. *How can I teach my puppy not to chase chickens?*

I wonder whether you mean your own chickens or other people's? If you mean your own chickens, all you have to do is take the puppy among them on a lead as much as possible. Should he attempt to get excited and frighten them, or make leaps at them, jerk him very sharply with the command "Leave." If a puppy grows accustomed to chickens, cats, other dogs, and people, he will not be a nuisance with any of them.

If you have no chickens yourself, I can't see where your puppy is going to chase them. Surely you can't be the sort of owner who lets a puppy free among livestock? You should always keep the puppy either on a long cord or a lead where there are chickens, cattle, goats, or sheep. An animal with horns can do terrible damage to a puppy, and unless your puppy obeys the command "Leave, heel" instantly, it may run up purely out of curiosity to talk to a cow. This goes for a horse, too. People sometimes stop to talk to a child on a pony and let their puppy sniff the pony's heels; in a second the pony can kick and kill the puppy.

With animals, always look on the black side. It is no good saying after something awful has happened, "Oh, I didn't think it would do that." Most dog fights are caused because people don't anticipate their dog's reactions to the other dog in time to correct him. You must always be one step ahead of a dog.

If you are really desperate, find someone who is going to kill a chicken. Put your dog on a long cord and let him be present at the killing. When the chicken is dead, it will flap its wings and legs and cause the dog to get very excited. Let the dog go for the chicken, then pull it in by the cord, and beat it hard with the dead chicken. It will get such a fright it will never do it again.

Children and Puppies. *My puppy bites my little girl quite badly sometimes. She doesn't seem to mind, but I am frightened that as he grows bigger, he will really hurt her.*

You are absolutely right. A puppy that is allowed to nip when he feels like it may ultimately turn into a biting dog. The best thing to do with very young children and a new puppy is to supervise their play. When the puppy shows signs of being tired of being mauled about, take it away and put it in its indoor kennel to sleep. Remember, small puppies need an awful lot of sleep. At six weeks old they should not be out of their sleeping quarters for more than three hours a day, and that should be in small bouts at a time. The child should never be allowed to interfere with a resting puppy or grown dog. Its kennel or basket should be private, so that it can feel that when it is there, it is free from being interfered with or annoyed.

Children don't mean to annoy a puppy, but they like carrying it about, which few puppies like; the children draw their hands up to escape its nips, and that makes the puppy jump up, as it may think they are playing. It then gets smacked for jumping up and it ends up quite bewildered.

You do not say how old your little girl is. But any child over about six years old should be able to be very useful in the training of a puppy. If you eventually take the puppy to training classes, try to take the child along, too. My own little girl, when she was six years old, trained her four-month-old Black-and-Tan Terrier with very little help from me. It was lovely to watch the two of them performing in competitive obedience against German Shepherds and other larger dogs. By all means, let the child help to feed the puppy. If it does not pull on the lead, let her hold it when you are out walking in a safe district. Never, however, let her hold the lead when the puppy is in the town. It might suddenly get a fright by another dog and might snatch its lead free. If it got run over as a result, the child would never get over it. Not only that, but, unless she keeps it properly under control, a child and a dog in shops and crowded streets can be a nuisance to others. Remember everyone doesn't like children and dogs.

The puppy should be firmly scolded by the parents of the child if it does lose its temper and attempt to bite the child. It won't grow out of these things; it will grow worse if not corrected while still young. It should have bones given to it, and they should be taken away with the command "Give," and then given back again. If the puppy shows signs of growling or biting when this is done, it should be scolded in a very cross voice. But remember that the child must not be allowed to tease it by taking its bone away every time the puppy is enjoying it. When you really wish to take it away, do so quickly and firmly.

Get the puppy accustomed to having its mouth opened when it picks up something you don't wish it to have. This opening of the mouth will help in later life when you wish to give it medicine.

Chocolate. *My Poodle puppy adores chocolate. Will it hurt him?*

Chocolate in any quantity is extremely bad for dogs, but an occasional piece won't do any harm.

Bribery in training is a thing I recommend for small puppies; in this way an occasional chocolate drop works wonders. I did know one lady, however, who laid a track of chocolate drops from her house over the fields and back again to her house while out walking. She assured me that this was the only way she could get her dog to come home. Don't copy this bad habit; your puppy would get ill and very disobedient. When I say "chocolate," I also include cocoa, chocolate cookies, ices, and ice cream, blancmange and, most important of all, chocolate toffees, which can choke a puppy.

Choke Chains. *It seems awfully cruel to me to put a young puppy on a choke chain and correct it for pulling. After all, it is only young once.*

I think you are being oversentimental; a puppy cannot enjoy pulling on a lead. Think of the weight he is pulling compared with his own size. A puppy should be taught from the age of twelve weeks to wear a thick-linked choke chain, the cost of which is very small. They range in size from 12 to 26 inches, although you can have any size made to order. The way to measure the length is to take a piece of string or tape and measure around under the dog's chin and up over his ears, then allow 2 inches extra for getting it over the head and for growth. They should always have two or three links hanging free on the pulling end of the choke chain.

The thin-linked variety are not so kind, and as one has to snatch hard at the lead to correct a pulling puppy, you do need the thick links to prevent any bruising. There is no pain for a dog on a choke chain, only breathlessness, if it is not released quickly enough. It should never be tight; the dog should be jerked back and instantly loosed. If the jerk and the simultaneous command are sharp enough, then the puppy must learn in a few minutes. Anyone who says choke chains are cruel if used correctly is ignorant. They are only used to prevent injury to ears and neck, which results from the use of a leather collar. Leather collars that run with a ring on them are useless for training, and so are braces.

I think it is high time the term "choke chain" was changed to "check chain." Its purpose is to check the dog kindly. It is only used to choke him temporarily if he bites or is fighting.

Choking. *I have a horror of my puppy choking. She swallows her food without chewing it, which terrifies me. What should I do if she does choke?*

If she is a small dog and is choking, the best thing to do is to pick her up, hold her upside down, and shake her, hoping to dislodge whatever was stuck. Occasionally, however, a dog swallows and inhales a piece of meat; then the only thing to do is to make your little finger into a crook and try to hook up the offending piece of meat. Under no circumstances push it downward. Occasionally a puppy inhales a marble or some other object into the bronchioles and, if this happens, an X ray will reveal it. The object can then be removed by a bronchoscope inserted into the bronchiole. This, of course, is a vet's job.

A bone may scratch the throat and cause a puppy to cough and choke in an effort to relieve the pain, but the more he coughs, the worse he becomes. The only treatment is to give a sedative until the worst of the pain has worn off.

It is amazing what a puppy can swallow. Any vet can show you a museum of objects he has retrieved from dogs' stomachs—sharp things like glass and nails and even tennis balls. My own dog once swallowed a live rat whole. Luckily there were no ill effects.

If you have managed to retrieve a piece of meat that was choking your dog, remember that the throat will probably be sore and swollen for a day or two, so keep the puppy on a soft diet of bread and milk, or with an occasional egg. The white of an egg whipped up in milk is always a safe and soothing diet; a teaspoonful of honey adds nourishment and is soothing to an inflamed surface.

As you have this horror of choking, I advise you to cut up or grind your puppy's meat very small; then there is very little risk of its choking. Do not let your puppy get hold of a ball of string or wool. The string can get caught around its tongue and the wool fluff can be inhaled, causing pneumonia or bronchitis.

Coat (Natural). *When do puppies get their permanent coat? My three-month-old puppy still has a very poor coat. As she is a Shetland Sheepdog, I am hoping she will have a lovely long-haired one.*

A puppy begins to change his baby coat for a permanent adult one at about three months old and is fully in coat by eight months. It is essential to provide all the vitamins and minerals your puppy needs to develop a good coat. Also the temperature of the puppy's surroundings make a lot of difference. A good heavy coat is developed more quickly when a puppy is kept outside than when it is always in the warmth of the house.

Be careful not to brush the puppy with too stiff a brush; you can make her bite by not being gentle enough. Until her permanent coat comes through, your puppy hardly needs brushing. But to accustom her to it, a hound brush, worn on the hand, is the best thing.

Boiled linseed improves the texture of the coat and gives it a wonderful shine. Many show people feed their dogs with some boiled linseed before starting their show career. The linseed should be boiled in water until it forms a jelly when cold. A tablespoonful of the jelly a day is about right for a medium-sized puppy over six months old. I would not feed it to one any younger as it is inclined to make the puppy's bowels loose. The seeds of the linseed must be strained off, allowing only the liquid to come through the muslin you are using as a strainer.

Some puppies will have an undercoat and an overlength coat, which is waterproof. German Shepherds have this double-texture coat. That is why they are suitable as shepherd dogs, as the weather does not affect them so much. Some puppies, like the Mexican Hairless, have no coat at all. Short-coated dogs are far easier to keep clean than long-coated ones, but they feel the cold much more. It is essential to keep a long-haired puppy's coat free from tangles. This applies especially to Old English Sheepdogs. Once the coat is really matted, it is extremely difficult to comb it out. Long-haired dogs should have a regular brushing and combing from an early age. This also applies to dogs like the Yorkshire Terrier and Shih Tzu.

Coats (Artificial). *Should my puppy wear a coat in winter?*

There is no hard and fast rule about this. If the weather is wet and the puppy very young, it should not be out for longer than is necessary for it to fulfill its toilet functions. But if you have to take it for a walk in inclement weather, a waterproof coat is a great asset. Very tiny puppies should not go for walks anyway. Puppies with long, natural coats are best protected from the wet, but do not feel the cold so much. You just have to use your common sense about putting a coat on your puppy.

Dogs should grow up reasonably hardy. On the other hand, most diseases start off with a bad chill, which allows the germs to get a hold on the body. If chilling can be avoided by a coat, by all means, put one on the puppy. One can now buy waterproof bootees for dogs of all sizes, as well as waterproof coats and hats. So if you really want to keep your puppy warm and dry, you can do so in all weathers!

The main thing to consider is whether you are taking it for a quick brisk walk or waiting about at bus stops in the biting wind or rain, or gossiping in a street. In ordinary weather I doubt if the puppy needs a coat at all.

Collar. *At what age should my puppy wear a collar? I have braces on him at present.*

You are piling up trouble for yourself by using braces on your puppy. They cause a dog to pull on the lead and have a bad effect on the shoulders of the puppy if you want him for show. There is no reason at all why a puppy shouldn't wear a collar from about seven weeks old. The rolled leather ones are the lightest and do not damage the coat. Pay no attention if the puppy scratches and obviously wishes to get rid of the collar; he will soon get used to it.

Constipation. *My puppy is terribly constipated. I give him plenty of bones. What else can I do?*

Stop the bones. Puppies can get dangerously constipated by eating too many bones. This can cause a tear at the anus, and great pain to the puppy. Milk is a laxative, as is brown

bread. Give just soft foods for a day or two, and this
condition will soon right itself. Big marrow bones are excellent for the puppy to gnaw, but anything he can eat right up
is dangerous.

You can cause a complete stoppage by constipating the
puppy too much with bones. Then an operation for the
relief of the stoppage has to be performed. Occasionally
stones eaten by the puppy cause a stoppage. If the puppy
seems quiet and in pain or cries when he tries to make a
bowel movement, take him to the vet straight away. The
trouble with puppies is they will eat everything that comes
their way—pieces of coal, wood, even spools of thread—and
their intestines have an awful job dealing with these unnatural foreign bodies.

Corns. *I saw a dog recently with large corns on its elbows.
What does this come from, and how shall I prevent my
puppy from getting them?*

Heavy dogs get these from lying on concrete. The way to
avoid such things is to give the puppy a nice soft bed of
blankets or a sprung chair. I have never seen a young dog
with corns.

Cow Hocks. *My puppy's hocks turn inward. What can I do
to improve this? He looks very ugly from the back.*

Cow hocks are often a hereditary factor in the dog; but
when a puppy like a Great Dane is growing very fast, it
doesn't put on much weight and the thighs, or "stifles" to
give them the correct name, do not carry much flesh. This
causes the hocks to turn inward. As the puppy gets adult
and puts on weight, this will improve to a certain extent.
Some breeds, noticeably St. Bernards and Great Pyrenees,
tend to have "bad hocks," and one should be most careful
to choose one with sound hocks, for you are unlikely to win
in the show ring with a puppy that has cow hocks.

Never overexercise a dog of a heavy breed when it is

young. It will tend to have bow legs and cow hocks if you do. A puppy exercises itself quite enough by running about the house. Even a grown-up St. Bernard needs no more than a mile of walking a day. All these heavy breeds are much better let loose in a field to play about to their heart's content; they then stop when they feel tired.

Cysts. *My Collie has a lump on her shoulder. It doesn't seem to hurt her, and I can lift it up in the skin. What do you think it is?*

This is probably a sebaceous cyst that has formed in the skin. They consist of the fatty secretion of the skin and they are benign. Occasionally they break, and masses of butterlike substance can be squeezed out. When they break, there is always a risk of infection. If the cyst is very unsightly or in any way handicaps the puppy, the vet can remove it for you with a local anesthetic. If it does none of these things, however, I suggest you leave well enough alone. Cysts have a habit of returning again and again. Some dogs, in old age, become a mass of them.

My own Dane had a big one on her shoulder; this formed where she had had her distemper inoculation. That is why I suggest this inoculation should be done in the flank.

Interdigital cysts are infected ones caused by a streptococcal infection, and must not be mixed up with the benign cysts we have been discussing. (See "Blebs.")

Dandruff. *My puppy has dandruff in his coat. What should I do for him?*

Dandruff is contagious inasmuch as he probably caught it from his mother. A good medicated dog soap cures this, but the soap should be dried in, not rinsed out. Dachshunds, English Toy Terriers, and similar breeds with short coats are far more likely to have dandruff than the long-coated breeds. A good brushing every day stimulates the pores of the skin and helps to overcome this mild infection.

Deafness. *I think my Dalmation puppy is deaf, although he is only four months old. Is this possible?*

Yes, occasionally one does get a puppy born deaf, and usually it is in breeds like Dalmatians or Harlequin Great Danes. Many people think their dogs are deaf, when, in reality, the puppy is just not listening. Only an expert could really tell you whether in fact it is deaf or merely not interested in your voice.

Deafness may be caused by wax in the ear. It is well worthwhile to have the puppy's ears examined by a vet before assuming he is deaf. I have trained deaf puppies to obey me on signal alone, but it needs a puppy to be intensely fond of its owner to get this response. Beagles are such stubborn little dogs that they often appear deaf when in fact they are concentrating on scents and simply don't hear their owners' voices or other sounds.

Death. *My puppy ran out onto the road and got killed by a car. It looked so natural, I wasn't sure it was dead. How can I be sure when a dog is dead?*

When an animal dies, the ceasing of the heartbeat is said to be death, but puppies have been born that are apparently dead and have been discarded, only to be found later breathing. With a road accident, however, one can only be really sure at first by holding a piece of cold glass to the puppy's nose, and if after two or three minutes it doesn't fog up, then the puppy is dead. Another way to test for life is to touch the puppy's eyeball; if this doesn't cause the eyelids to flutter, the puppy is dead.

A deeply unconscious dog can have such shallow breathing that it is practically imperceptible. Only when heart and respiration have really ceased can an animal be said to be dead.

Should a puppy survive such an accident, it is essential to treat it for shock. Wrap it up in a blanket and put two covered hot-water bottles on either side of its ribs. A few drops of brandy on its tongue will often work wonders. Call the vet at once.

Defiance. *My puppy growls furiously at me if I dare to take his piece of damp rag away. He adores this floor cloth out of the kitchen bucket and treats it as though it were his own puppy. How can I get it from him and teach him to give it up when I want it?*

Put his lead or a piece of string on the puppy's collar. When he growls defiance at you, pick up the lead and draw him toward you. Grab the piece of cloth firmly in both your hands on either side of his mouth and with a quick jerk, yank it sharply toward the floor with the word "give." The puppy has to open its mouth if the rag is jerked downward over its tongue. Praise it immediately you have got it away, and give it back to him. Repeat the treatment as often as is necessary to teach him that the word "give" means let go. Always protect your hands with thick gloves before doing any of these corrective exercises. You must not get bitten or you will feel furious. A furious owner is never a good one from the training point of view.

Puppies sometimes get under chairs or beds and growl defiance at their owners. Treat this in a similar manner. If you can anticipate the problem, attach a long piece of cord to his collar so that you can pull him out with a sharp jerk, and then praise him. A puppy always knows when he is defeated.

Destructiveness. *My Boxer puppy is terribly destructive. What can I do to stop this?*

Well, there are many ways of stopping this destructive habit. First, you can confine the puppy in an indoor kennel when no one is about to watch it. Second, you can muzzle it, which I don't like, and, third—a much better way than either of these—you can give up a certain amount of time each day to playing with the puppy and giving it obedience training so that its young mind is occupied fruitfully. Puppies cannot just grow up by themselves. A puppy is nearly as big a responsibility as a new baby.

If you give the puppy lots of playthings like old socks and shoes and large marrow bones, it will amuse itself for a long time. But when it gets bored on its own, you must be ready to play with it and tire it out, or else put it safely in its bed where it can do no damage. Most of this tearing up of things is due to teething, and to inquisitiveness—the puppy tries everything with its teeth.

As the male puppy gets sexually adult, he will pass through a stage of sexual frustration, and the tearing up of things is all part of this. The quickest cure for this is castration, which I think is best done at about seven months old.

Dogs are far more destructive than bitches. In fact, I think bitches are far nicer to own anyway. I can't imagine why people will choose dogs—they fight more, destroy things more, and are far more difficult to train. The twenty-eight days or so in a year when a bitch is in heat are not nearly so troublesome as owning a male dog who is forever interested in the other sex.

Dewclaws. *I have a Great Pyrenees puppy with three dewclaws on each leg. People tell me dewclaws should be taken off all puppies before they leave the breeder. Shall I have these removed by a vet?*

No, the dewclaws on a Great Pyrenees dog, if it is wanted as a show dog, must remain on. It is part of the breed standard; why, I cannot imagine, as they are unsightly and dangerous. I would, however, have them removed by your vet if the dog is only wanted as a pet. They can easily get torn off, and if the dog jumps up at its owner at all, they can catch in his clothes.

If dewclaws aren't removed, they must be kept short, so that they do not hook over. The removal of dewclaws when the dog is older is not a serious operation. After the vet has removed them, the place should be kept clean with an adhesive bandage dressing, which is left on for about ten days, until the stitches are removed. A small puppy doesn't need stitches.

Diarrhea. *My eight-week-old puppy has developed diarrhea. What shall I do for it?*

I conclude you have just bought this puppy? If so, the change of routine and food is quite likely to give it diarrhea. This usually passes off in a couple of days. I should call the vet if at all prolonged or if the puppy has a temperature. Otherwise a bismuth mixture, as for children, bought from the druggist is perfectly safe. The puppy being equal in weight to a month-old baby, the usual dose is a teaspoonful of medicine every four hours. The old-fashioned remedy of arrowroot instead of its ordinary milk is still quite good. You can replace its food for a day or two with a fortified milk substitute, as with these products no other food is necessary. They have all the ingredients necessary for complete nourishment. In concentrated form, they can either be made with water or milk. If a puppy has diarrhea, I would use water, changing to milk as the puppy recovers. Then slowly get it back onto its normal diet with scraped shin of beef and a little brown bread.

If the puppy has any other symptoms except diarrhea, looks listless, and doesn't want to eat, call the vet at once. A puppy's life always hangs by a thread when it is young; it is never wise to wait until serious symptoms develop.

Be sure the puppy is wormed twice before it is three months old. Worms can cause loose bowel movements.

Diet. *How should I feed my eight-week-old puppy?*

You do not mention the breed of your puppy, so it is not easy to give you a hard and fast diet.

A diet, to be adequate and complete, must contain the right amount of fat, protein, and starch, as well as all the vitamins needed by the body to make growth and impart good health to the puppy.

There are a great number of different ways of feeding puppies. I shall give you two or three to guide you. You must use your common sense as to quantities and vary them to suit your particular puppy.

There are three main ways to bring up a puppy. The first is an ordinary household diet of warm cow's milk, scraped beef, and brown bread, coupled with an occasional egg and vitamins such as A and D in the form of cod-liver oil, or the addition of multivitamin capsules, or a complete mineral and vitamin supplement in the form of Vionate. The second is a diet provided by manufacturers of dogfoods, which consists of canned meat and puppy meal (changing to dog meal or biscuits as the puppy grows older), with the addition of cow's milk. The third is a natural diet consisting of raw beef, wholemeal biscuits, and carrot and grass meal, with the addition of seaweed and natural minerals.

All the diets are basically the same, supplying milk, cereals, and meat.

Some people try to rear their dogs on a vegetarian diet, but dogs' digestions are made to deal with meat; dogs are carnivorous, not herbivorous, animals, and therefore these diets must be unsuitable for puppies.

The quantities given in the following diets are for puppies of eight to ten weeks, weighing when adult about 25 pounds. Larger or smaller breeds must have larger or smaller amounts in proportion.

Appetite is the greatest guide to feeding. If anything is left on the puppy's dish after eating, it is being overfed and should have the next meal reduced accordingly. A puppy should always be willing to eat more after its meal, but should not be given more than the right amount. The right amount of daily intake is about one-half ounce per pound body weight. This must of necessity be a rough guide.

The larger breeds like Great Danes could not be fed this way as their rate of growth is so quick.

All puppies of eight weeks old should have five meals per day. See the diet that follows.

Most people nowadays use Pablum, or fortified milk substitutes to start their new puppies off. I use the milk substitute for one meal and milk as a drink at all others, and meat for three meals. The meat should be scraped beef unless a canned meat is used. Lamb or mutton, veal, and pork are not so good.

A puppy's digestion is judged by its bright eye, its normal formed stools, its clean-smelling breath, and its gaiety. A dull, listless puppy is a wrongly fed or ill puppy.

Eating earth and stones is due to either a mineral deficiency or worms. Correctly fed puppies don't eat earth or manure.

HOUSEHOLD DIET

6:30 a.m.	Warm milk and a fortified milk substitute or Pablum, about a dessertspoonful to a tablespoonful according to age and size
10:30 a.m.	2 ounces scraped beef, drink of milk
2:30 p.m.	Brown bread and milk
6:00 p.m.	Scraped beef and Cornflakes or bread, drink of milk
10:00 p.m.	Drink of milk

As the puppy gets bigger, drop the milk substitute, which is a complete food, and add one more meal of scraped beef.

At twelve weeks the meals will be reduced to four a day, then three, and at six months they will be reduced to two. By this age a puppy of Spaniel size would be having 1/2 pound of raw beef per day, plus four slices of brown bread or two cupfuls of biscuit meal, soaked in boiling water or gravy and allowed to cool before feeding, and a drink of milk.

A Great Dane at six months old should be having one pound of meat per day, one pint of milk, six slices of brown bread, biscuits, or Cornflakes. A Dane never needs more than one and one-half pounds of meat per day; bread or biscuits are given according to appetite and condition.

All puppies need the addition of vitamins and minerals to their diet to assist teething and growth.

If a puppy scratches, the diet should be changed as the puppy is possibly allergic to something in the diet, or is being overfed. A bad-tempered puppy is usually one that has indigestion—usually due to overfeeding. Tidbits are enjoyed by puppies but are not good for them in any quantity. The puppy's saliva runs at mealtimes, so punctuality is of paramount importance. If you are traveling with a puppy, it is better to take canned meat than fresh meat. Milk should be taken in a bottle and if necessary boiled before the journey to keep it from going sour. Goat's milk can be fed to puppies, but it has a higher fat content than cow's milk and therefore may not be so well tolerated.

Puppies should not be allowed to beg for food at the owners' mealtimes. Household scraps can be given to adult dogs but are unsuitable for growing puppies.

GENERAL GUIDE FOR FEEDING MEDIUM-SIZED
DOGS WEIGHING FROM TWENTY TO THIRTY
POUNDS WHEN ADULT.
SMALLER OR LARGER BREEDS IN PROPORTION.

8-12 Weeks

7:30 a.m.	Drink of warm cow's milk
9:30 a.m.	1 1/2 ounces of fresh or canned meat and 1/2 cup puppy meal or two slices of brown bread soaked in meat stock
3:00 p.m.	Drink of milk with brown bread or a puppy biscuit

6:00 p.m.   1 1/2 ounces minced beef cooked or raw or canned meat with Cornflakes or half a cupful of soaked puppy meal

10:00 p.m.   Drink of warm milk

12 Weeks to 6 Months

7:30 a.m.   Drink of cow's milk, two toasted slices of brown bread with butter or a few biscuits or puppy meal

12 noon   2-4 ounces canned meat or minced cooked beef or fish

6:00 p.m.   2-4 ounces fresh or canned meat mixture with dry brown bread or half a cup of puppy meal soaked beforehand. A drink of milk.

6 Months Onward

As a dog reaches six months, feedings are gradually reduced to two a day, 1/2 pound of beef, or one small can of dog meat, and about a cup of dog meal and a drink of milk should keep a dog healthy, providing vitamins are added to the diet in some form.

NATURAL FEEDING
by Newman Turner

Puppy Diet to 4 Months

Allow puppies to remain on the bitch for as long as possible, weaning at from 8-10 weeks. While they are still on the bitch at from 3-4 weeks of age, offer each puppy a thin gruel of tree-barks powder (mixtures of nutritious tree barks are now in most pet shops) and milk, mixed with a little honey, starting once daily and gradually increasing to four meals a day. Introduce also one meal of scraped or minced raw meat. Then, at weaning give more solid food to make a quantity up to about one-tenth of the weight of the puppy, but let appetite be the real measure. Feed at regular times; see that each puppy has enough to satisfy his appetite in a few minutes, then remove anything left over. Allow nothing else (except fresh water) till next meal. Where more than one puppy (especially in a litter) are being fed give them individual dishes or feed each puppy separately. Suggested times:

7:00-8:00 a.m. A liquid meal. Use raw, unpasteurized milk, with the addition of a little honey (start with a teaspoonful for a young puppy, and increase to a dessertspoonful as he gets older). Make this into a fluid gruel by adding powdered tree barks (slippery elm, white willow, dill, etc.) or pure slippery elm (not the "slippery elm foods" containing flour and sugar). Start with 1 teaspoonful and increase gradually to 1 dessertspoonful of the powder.

Noon-1:00 p.m. A meal of raw ground cereals (not packeted breakfast foods, but wholewheat flour, oatmeal, bean meal, with fruit and olive oil. I use Herb-Royal Junior Rearing Food which is a good raw mixture specially prepared for this purpose. Use also a wholemeal Puppy Meal as the pup gets older, first mixing with, or alternating with, the puppy rearing food, then at 3-4 months the puppy biscuit meal may be fed straight. Soak both in milk, or vegetable water, flavored with a little yeast extract. Add some olive oil (a few drops for a very small puppy, increasing to a teaspoonful). As often as possible add some fruit, dried and fresh, such as chopped raisins or sultanas, or grated raw apple. Soft fruits may also be used in season, particularly blackberries, currants and raspberries, according to the puppy's taste. These supply valuable vitamins, particularly C. An alternative is a little black-currant juice or puree.

3:30 p.m.-4:00 p.m. Raw meat (half the day's ration)—about 2 ounces for the young puppy shredded but not minced (except in the very early pre-weaning stage). For this meal feed the meat alone, merely sprinkled with a little seaweed powder and olive oil. Never mix with any cereals.

7:00-8:00 p.m. Raw meat (half the day's ration). See 3:30-4:00 p.m. for quantity. Shred it with a knife—do not mince it. The puppy's stomach muscles need the exercise provided by chunks of meat. Give larger pieces as the puppy grows older, up to hen-egg size for the larger adult dog. Add to the meat up to a teaspoonful of cod-liver oil or olive oil.

For roughage and valuable fresh vitamins, chop finely up to a good dessertspoonful of raw vegetables: parsley, dandelion leaves, cress, mint, onion, celery-tops, and some grated carrot. Fine chopping is necessary because dogs do not easily digest cellulose, as they cannot chew their food. The leaves of wild garlic are also very valuable. Whether or not you can always manage the chopped vegetables always add a sprinkle of seaweed powder and a little garlic or garlic tablet. Seaweed is unique in providing minerals and all known trace elements which are so essential to prevent dietary deficiencies. Garlic is the best natural source of sulphur and the most effective preventive against disease.

Large raw bones should be given after some of the meat feeds—the puppy will be doing good to his teeth and stimulate the digestive processes. Raw, minced herrings, which contain valuable oils and other elements derived from the sea, may be used occasionally in place of the meat at one of the meals. Break a raw egg over a meat feed occasionally if you wish—but not more often than twice or three times a week.

Every day give a tablet of garlic. This not only helps to prevent disease and worms, but supplies other valuable ingredients to tone up the system.

4 Months Onward

After 4 months, cut out the early fluid meals and give one cereal and two meat meals. Cereal (rearing food and/or puppy meal) at midday; raw meat afternoon and evening.

At 6-7 Months

At 6-7 months, cut down the meals to two a day—the cereal meal should be given at midday, and the main, meat meal in the evening. Again, regularity is necessary and 12 noon and 6 p.m. are ideal times.

Thus, by 7 months, you will arrive at the Adult Diet. This consists of one meal of cereal, with the supplements advised for puppies, except that the oil may be omitted. Vary the fluid with which you moisten the cereal, the cereal itself, and the fruit that goes with it.

For the meat meal, vary the type of meat. You can use such things as sheeps' or calves' heads—eyes, brains and all. You should often give raw bones—and don't believe those who say they are harmful. Cooked bones, however, are deadly—avoid them like the plague, whatever kind they are. You can get from the knacker or butcher sometimes what is known as meat "in the bone"—i.e., a flank of sheep, with the meat still on the ribs. Dogs love these. You may give some liver or kidneys with the meat from time to time. but a lot of offal for the domesticated dog cannot be recommended. Raw chopped rabbits can be given whole—fur, bones and everything. Raw herrings are one of the best alternatives to meat. For the adult dog, slice across the fish in chunks about 1/2 in. to 1 in. thick, bones and all—but remove the head and tail.

A Treebarks Blend for making the first gruel for weaning and a Junior Rearing food for young puppies as their first cereal food (i.e., ready-mixed raw oatmeal, wheatmeal, carrot meal, bean meal, grass meal, milk, and malt, etc.) is stocked by the big stores like Harrods, Selfridges, and most pet shops. Supplies are also available from Herb Royal Ltd., Bridgwater, Somerset [England], who also stock the herbal supplements.

Disk. *Do puppies get slipped disks? My Dachshund has seemed in pain when she moves, ever since she jumped for a ball.*

Yes, puppies and adult dogs certainly do get slipped disks. It is less likely in a puppy than an adult dog because their bones are soft and very flexible.

The first sign of a slipped disk is that the tail of the puppy is held in a most peculiar way, with a curve outward near the base of the tail. The end of the tail does not turn upward as does a normal puppy's; it hangs down straight or curves slightly inward. However much you play with the puppy, this tail carriage will not alter. If you suspect disk trouble in a small dog, catch hold of it by its tail near the base with the right hand, and supporting the body under the chest and forefeet, let it hang by its tail for a few seconds. It will probably struggle a bit, and this struggling, with the dog's spine extended, usually allows the disk to slip back into place. If the puppy is as big as a Retriever, one must catch the animal around the tummy under the right arm, supporting its chest with the left. This, I know, needs someone rather strong. Some pain-killers and muscle relaxants designed for human use can be very effective for dogs, too, with the dosage depending on weight; but all medicines of this type should really be taken under veterinary observation. Aspirins always relieve acute pain. The dog should not be exercised more than necessary. Once a puppy has had a disk displaced, it may happen again.

Distemper. *What are the symptoms of distemper?*

The first signs of distemper may only show as a dullness in the puppy—an unwillingness to play. Its nose may become hot, and there may be a greenish discharge from the eyes, which collects in the duct at the corner nearest the nose. There may also be a discharge from the nose. Diarrhea may be present, and in bad cases the puppy may have fits. Food is refused. As the disease gets worse, complications may set in such as pneumonia or bronchitis or both. The puppy will sneeze and cough and be generally miserable.

In some cases the puppy vomits, the tongue becomes ulcerated, and the mouth has a most unpleasant smell. The puppy has a great thirst and drinks vast quantities of water, which it immediately vomits. Stools are of a watery consistency and smell foul. It is this diarrhea that so weakens the puppy that usually it has not the strength to resist the infection and dies. Paralysis or fits are symptoms that develop late; if this occurs, there is little hope of saving the puppy.

With vaccination against distemper the puppy becomes immune in about three weeks, or if it does catch the disease, it is in such an attenuated form that it usually recovers without complications. A booster vaccine has to be given about once a year, and some people give one before a dog show. The risk of disease at shows cannot be emphasized enough.

Treatment: The puppy should be kept in a warm room at an even temperature. A jacket should be made for the puppy to keep it warm (see "Pneumonia"). Plenty of drinking water should be available. All other dogs should be isolated from it. Bedding that is soiled should be burned and the owner's hands washed after each contact with the dog to stop spread of infection.

The diet should be very light and digestible. Bulky foods should not be given. Fortified milk substitutes and nutrient supplements, the white of an egg, beef tea, etc., are all good. A little of what the puppy fancies always does more good than trying to force food it doesn't want down its throat.

Its temperature should be taken twice a day in the rectum so that when the vet calls, you can tell him what it was when you took it. After each use, let the thermometer stand in a glass of mild antiseptic. Aspirin at the rate of 3/4 grain per pound of body weight can be given every four hours or until the vet prescribes otherwise.

The discharge from the eyes must be continually bathed away with Optrex or boracic acid solution, and the nose likewise; otherwise the caked discharge produces a raw, ulcerated surface. On no account take the puppy out in winter to perform its functions, unless it absolutely refuses to perform elsewhere. If it does go out for a few minutes, it must have a woolen coat that completely covers its chest as well as its back.

Even when the puppy is well, great care must be taken to keep it from overexertion and from catching a chill, until at least ten days to two weeks have elapsed. Occasionally distemper will leave a puppy with paralysis or fits, in which case, in my opinion, it is better to put the puppy to sleep. A few dogs have been known to recover the use of their limbs, but very few.

Docking. *My Corgi puppy has no tail at all. Can I sue the breeder, as I wanted it for show?*

I doubt if you can sue the breeder for this since the taillessness of your Corgi may be quite normal. Many Corgis are born this way. The American Kennel Club recognizes two Corgi breeds: Cardigan Welsh Corgis and Pembroke

Welsh Corgis. The standard for Pembroke Corgis says "tail—short, preferably natural." I doubt if you would lose any points at all in a show because your puppy's tail was too short. If it were too long, it might spoil the puppy's chances.

In breeds where docking is called for by the standard, all tails should be docked before the puppies' eyes are open and should be done by an expert. The incision must be between two vertebrae, and the stumps should be dabbed with tincture of benzoin compound to stop bleeding and to disinfect the bleeding tip. The bitch should be taken away so that she cannot see the docking process. She will lick the puppies frantically when she comes back. Don't worry if they bleed a little; it soon stops.

Always consult the breed standard before attempting to dock puppies' tails. Even vets aren't always conversant with this. It is far better to get an experienced breeder who shows dogs to dock the puppies' tails for you, unless docking by anyone other than a veterinarian is prohibited in your state.

Dosing. *How should I dose my puppy? She struggles terribly if I try to give her cod-liver oil.*

As far as possible, all puppies should have their medicines given to them in pill form, so that the pills can be wrapped up in a piece of meat, which is swallowed without being chewed. If, however, you must give liquid medicine, the best way to give it is by holding the loose lip of the mouth at the side away from the gums; there is a distinct pocket when you do this. Then tilt the puppy's head slightly, and slowly pour the fluid. If the puppy won't swallow, stroke its throat until it does, keeping the head slightly tilted. Should the puppy show the slightest sign of coughing or choking, lower its head at once.

Pills can be easily placed on the back of the tongue and the mouth held gently closed until the puppy has swallowed them. This method is used when the puppy is refusing its food and you cannot, therefore, put the pill in its meat.

Most worm cures these days are made in pill form, and as the puppy doesn't need starving before dosing for worms, as it did with the old-fashioned cures, it is easy to give it the dose in its food.

Always be very careful to read about the dosage before giving medicine to a puppy. I always check the dosage each time—it is so easy to slip up—and with a young puppy an overdose could have tragic results.

If a puppy's mouth has been handled often, the giving of medicine should be easy.

Dribbling. *My puppy is a perpetual dribbler. What is the cause?*

Without hearing more about this, it is impossible to diagnose the cause of excessive salivating. Car sickness is one cause; feeling generally sick is another. There is also an excessive secretion of saliva when there is a nonspecific painful condition of the mucus inside the mouth, but this is unusual in puppies.

I am wondering whether you have only noticed this dribbling at mealtimes—either yours or the puppy's? If so, it is quite normal. I have seen a puppy's saliva run like a tap when I am preparing its meal. This is Nature's way of providing the secretion necessary for the digestion of the meal and does not indicate any trouble. I recently saw a Newfoundland at Crufts with a bib on; he was dribbling so much with excitement that he was ruining his nicely brushed coat.

Occasionally inflammation of the parotid gland produces a swelling like mumps in a dog, and this causes the saliva to run. Should there be any swelling in the neck or tongue, you should consult your vet at once.

Saliva runs copiously in rabies and, in countries where rabies exist, any drooling dog should be suspect.

Drinking. *How much water should my Labrador puppy need per day? He is always drinking.*

There can be no hard and fast rule about the quantity of water a puppy should drink. You should always leave clean water in a place he knows so that he can help himself. If he is thirsty, he will drink water; if he is not thirsty, he will be satisfied with his drinks of milk.

Any excess fluid is passed off by the kidneys. It is far more dangerous for a puppy to drink too little than too much, as he could get dehydrated, which would lead him to having a dry, hot nose, a dull eye, and lusterless coat. All animals thrive much better with water ad lib. Do not let the drinking water be freezing cold with ice on it. It should be roughly at room temperature. I always place the drinking trough on a baking tin, as most puppies are rather sloppy drinkers and splash the carpet.

If a puppy is ill, it can live on clean drinking water alone for quite a time; never force food down a puppy's throat. A puppy with kidney trouble will drink an excessive amount of water, but it is a rare thing indeed for a puppy to have kidney trouble unless it has caught a severe chill.

Ears. *My puppy's ears will not stand up as they should. Is there any method of assisting them to become erect?*

Yes, puppies' ears can be "trained" to stand erect by taping them with adhesive tape. Professional dog handlers know all the tricks of the trade, and you would be wise to take your dog along to one of these people and ask him to help you. The puppy should be about five or six months old when the ears are taped.

Teething makes a puppy's ears do all kinds of things not in accordance with the breed standards. Therefore one should never despair of a puppy's ears becoming correctly erect until teething has finished. Corgis, German Shepherds, and Terriers are the breeds that have the most trouble with ear carriage. Some breeds like Shetland Sheepdogs need weights on the tips of their ears to make them bend over, as do some Fox Terriers. Ear carriage is hereditary.

Exercise. *How much exercise should I give my five-month-old Scottie puppy?*

A lot of nonsense is talked about exercising dogs. People spend hours braving the elements in inclement weather in order to give their puppies masses of exercise. As long as a puppy is allowed the freedom of the home and is given one reasonable walk a day for about fifteen minutes, it will grow up perfectly all right. It is far more dangerous to overexercise than underexercise a puppy. This applies especially to large dogs like Wolfhounds, Great Danes, and St. Bernards. In fact, more puppies of these breeds have been spoiled by ignorant owners overexercising them than by giving them too little exercise. Ten minutes' freedom in a field is worth half an hour's walk on the roads, for the puppy dashes about freely.

Your Scottie puppy will be perfectly fit and well on half an hour's total exercise during the day. If you have time for more, after it has reached the age of four months, by all means give it more, but for health purposes it doesn't need it, provided it gets the freedom of the home for part of the day.

Eyes. *The lower lids of my puppies' eyes are very red. Is this all right?*

The eyes of a puppy should at all times be bright and clear, free from mucus, and the lids should not be baggy and bloodshot as they are in Bloodhounds. Bloodshot eyes are a Bloodhound characteristic, not a disease, unless they are running thick mucus at the same time.

The lids should be pale pink inside, and any redness must be looked upon with suspicion and the appropriate medication applied. Very young puppies may have slight mucus each day in the inner corner of the eye, which may be due to dust in the bedding or to too strong a light. A draft will produce running eyes; that is why all puppy beds should be raised off the floor.

All puppies are born with dark blue eyes. Their correct lifetime coloring will not develop until they are approximately three months old. Always choose a dark-eyed puppy if you can. It is well known that light-eyed puppies are likely to be "scatty." A dark eye is one of the points in most of the breed standards, as laid down by the American Kennel Club.

Inflammation of the eye should be treated at once by bathing it with Optrex or boracic acid powder dissolved in boiling water and allowed to cool. Always bathe from the inside toward the outer end of the eyelid. Never use the same piece of cotton for bathing both eyes, or you may spread infection. Should the eye not respond quickly to home treatment, get in touch with your vet, who will no doubt treat the condition with antibiotics. Sometimes an ingrowing eyelash may cause a lot of pain, and the condition has to be treated by an operation to remove an elliptical piece of skin on the inner side of the eyelid. This unfortunately leaves a scar.

The health of a puppy can be judged by his bright-eyed appearance. If your puppy has a dull eye, investigate his health.

Eczema. *My puppy has eczema. What can I do for it?*

This condition is nearly always caused by wrong diet. A change of diet often clears it up in a remarkable way.

Eczema can be of two kinds—the dry, and the moist (running or weeping) eczema. Both kinds are accompanied by violent irritation and scratching. Small red spots and, in bad cases, bare patches typify the complaint. It is often of an allergic nature, and antihistamine medicines often help to cure it. Treatment with a medicated soap, a change of diet, a light dosage of milk of magnesia every other day, and a soothing lotion on the infected parts usually clear it up.

Fever. *My puppy looks listless and is panting rather a lot. I am wondering whether he has a fever?*

A fever is always accompanied by a rise in temperature. The normal temperature is between 101.5°F. and 102°F.; anything much above 102° should be a warning that all is not well. If the weather is very hot, I have known healthy dogs' temperatures to rise to 105°F., but when put in the cool, they instantly reverted to normal as the dogs cool down.

The signs of a fever are dull eyes, a dry, hot nose, and an excessive thirst. Panting accompanies a fever, but a dog, of course, sweats through its tongue and nose, so it can be perfectly well and still be panting a lot.

Panting does not necessarily mean that the puppy is thirsty, but a thirsty puppy pants. This all sounds rather Irish!

The temperature of a puppy should always be taken by moistening the bulb of the thermometer with a little spit and placing it very gently into the rectum. It is easier if you have someone to help you hold the puppy. The thermometer should be inserted with a slightly circular motion and held firmly between your finger and thumb throughout the procedure. Wipe it clean and run it under the cold tap before putting it away. Always read the thermometer before taking the puppy's temperature in case someone hasn't shaken it down. It should be shaken down with a twist of the wrist. Few thermometers register correctly in the half-minute it says they register in. I always leave them in for at least one minute.

Fighting. *My new puppy and my old dog fight all day long. What can I do to stop them?*

The older dog is probably jealous of the new puppy, but even if he is, he must be made to tolerate it. It is not possible, at first, to teach a puppy to leave the older one alone; the puppy, being young, naturally wants to play. But if the older one can't stand it, he will have to be kept apart until the puppy grows old enough to be trained to "leave." It may be necessary to punish the older dog mildly if he retaliates by fighting when the puppy is a nuisance. After all, the law of the jungle is definitely that older animals do not go for baby ones.

If the puppy has had too much, it will lie on his back with his feet waving in the air, which means "pax" in animal language, and the older dog will respect this. I wouldn't worry unduly, unless the puppy or older dog is getting injured in this fighting. Dogs can look as if they are fighting when actually it is a form of play.

Taking the two dogs together in the car is a good way of introducing them, as they are occupied with the traveling and are unlikely to fight in a moving car. If they once sleep together, they will stop fighting.

It is always possible, if things become unbearable, to muzzle both the dogs or just the older one.

Fire. *My puppy loves to lie stretched out in front of the fire. Will this harm him?*

I think it is a bad thing to allow your puppy to take the best of the fire whether it harms him or not. There may come a day when he doesn't wish to be moved from that place and bites the owner who tries to shift him. I believe that all dogs should have their own kennel, chair, or basket and go to it when the family is in the room.

The fire is not good for the puppy's eyes, which are inclined to get inflamed from the radiant heat given off by a fire. Then, too, if the fire should send out sparks, the puppy could easily be blinded or injured. The change of temperature from very hot to cold when you take him outdoors, is also a reason for not lettting him lie in front of the fire. It is so easy to get a puppy chilled, with dire consequences.

Fish. *Should I give my puppy fish?*

By all means, give your puppy fish. Fish is rich in vitamins and is a change from meat, but do not give more than one meal of fish per day. When my own Dane was tiny, I gave her fish three times a week but not because I thought fish better than meat, just to ring a change. Also I think that fish is high in protein, which a large puppy needs.

Be very careful to choose fish without bones. Even small bones can be dangerous to a puppy, which seldom chews its food but bolts it whole. If you give too much fish, the oily content of it is inclined to make the puppy's bowels loose— and when house-training a puppy, you want to avoid this at all costs.

Fits. *My puppy has just had a fit. What was the cause?*

There are many different causes of fits in puppies. The usual ones are irritation of the gums due to teething, and irritation of the intestines by worms. Both these conditions are not serious and can be cured. The more serious cause of fits is distemper, when an encephalitis or chorea ensues. Only expert veterinary advice can help you in this case.

Occasionally, owing to an overtight collar, a puppy will faint. The treatment is, of course, to loosen the collar and lie the dog flat. Choke chains put on upside down can also cause the puppy to faint as he is being half-choked. Choke chains should always be put on so that the running end pulls in an upward direction, not a downward one; then the weight of the running end opens up the chain, allowing freedom to breathe.

Some puppies have hysteria, which produces fits, but the cause of this is unknown. A puppy that has constant fits is not a good proposition, and your vet may suggest that you have it put to sleep. Vitamin B complex in large doses is always worth trying, as experiments on rats lacking in this vitamin have proved that they have fits. But as all puppies should have vitamins given to them from the moment they come to your home, fits from this cause should not occur.

Worm the puppy three times from birth to six months old, and thereafter if any signs of parasites are seen in the stool. If fits continue, it may be worth having a laboratory examination of his stool to determine whether a tapeworm is present.

Flatulence. *Somebody has warned me that puppies sometimes die of flatulence. A friend said his Dane died before the vet could reach her. Can you enlighten me as to whether this is common and what symptoms and first-aid remedies are?*

This is not a common occurrence in puppies. In fact, I can't think of a single case I have heard of. It seems to affect adult dogs more than puppies. It is true that unless immediate relief is given surgically, this distension can kill a dog. If you ever get such severe flatulence in your puppy, the best first-aid remedy is to put a piece of common washing soda, about the size of a nut, down its throat. This makes it vomit, and with the vomiting comes away some of the wind that is causing the distension.

The main thing to prevent any tragedy's happening is always to watch a puppy for about half an hour after a meal. People who feed their dogs and put them away in their kennels do sometimes find them dead in the morning. Diagnosis is easy for the puppy or adult dog as it just gets fatter and fatter around the tummy until it literally bursts. But long before this you would notice the puppy was refusing to move and in obvious pain. His eyes would look strained, and his whole attitude would be one of dejection and misery. No one quite knows the cause of this distension, but it is thought to be of allergic origin. An antihistamine pill would perhaps save its life if the vet were out. If you were brave enough to plunge the tip of a very sharp kitchen knife into the abdomen to let the gas out, undoubtedly this is the one thing that would save the puppy's life if it was dying.

Fleas. *My puppy is forever scratching and nibbling at his coat. Has he got fleas, do you think?*

No one can guess whether a puppy has fleas, or lice for that matter, unless they are actually seen. But one can easily get them out by buying a small carton of insect powder at the druggist and rubbing it well into the coat. If you don't like using powder and if the weather is warm, get some pesticidal soap and wash the puppy in it, leaving the soap to dry in. This will kill all insects. Repeat in three days' time, in case eggs have hatched out.

Be sure to disinfect the puppy's bedding or he will get reinfected. A dusting of pesticide powder ensures that the kennel or basket is free from parasites. Fleas can be picked up time and time again from fields inhabited by chickens or other animals. Dogs infect one another, so a constant watch must be kept.

Follicular Mange. *What is follicular mange?*

Follicular mange is caused by a mite that is passed from the bloodstream of the mother into the puppies' bloodstream before birth. It appears in the form of tiny red papules on the tummy, the forehead, and the chest. They are intensely irritating, and puppies with follicular mange are eternally scratching.

If you pick up one of these papules and squeeze it, it oozes, and you can squeeze out the mite, which can be seen under a microscope. The vet will do this to confirm his diagnosis.

In the past, people have considered this complaint almost incurable. I have not found this the case. I have found that a good pesticidal soap cures it if you wash the puppy and leave the soap in. Sherley's, the dog medicine people, tell me they have now evolved a new cure as well. Their address is Ashe Laboratories, Guildford, England.

The breeds most likely to suffer with follicular mange are Boxers, English Toy Terriers, and Dachshunds; in fact, dogs with short coats including Doberman Pinschers, etc.

Follicular mange is not contagious. But it looks ugly, as it inevitably leaves the puppy with no hair where it is infected. Directly the mites have been killed, the hair grows again.

Foreign Bodies. *My Irish Wolfhound puppy nearly went mad scratching his ear after we had been walking in long grass. What could he have done to it?*

He probably got a hay seed in his ear. This sets up an intense irritation, and the inner ear swells, which causes acute pain. The best thing to do is to take the puppy at once to the vet, who will examine his ear with an auroscope.

Sometimes puppies get a foreign body of some sort in their eye. If this happens, don't probe about for it; no puppy will stay still if you try to do this. By far the best treatment is to drop in a little castor oil or Optrex with an eye dropper.

It is wise to get a vet to see that the puppy hasn't scratched its cornea, or blindness might ensue if it gets infected. Should the eye be very inflamed, some aureomycin, or antibiotic eye ointment, will tackle infection. But as these drugs are obtainable only with a prescription, nobody but a doctor or vet can get them for you.

Fractures. *My son trod on my Labrador puppy's foot. It seems very swollen, and the puppy is lame. What should I do for it?*

The first thing to do is to take it to a vet for an X ray. It is very easy to break a puppy's toe by treading on it. Until a puppy is about four months old, its bones are very soft, and bumps and bangs don't seem to affect them permanently; but after this age the bones get harder and are more likely to break or crack. Always apply a splint made from two pieces of wood placed on either side of the paw and bandaged into place to prevent further injury. First aid can be applied by making a cold compress of a pad of cotton soaked in water, or even Optrex, and a piece of plastic over the top, and then a bandage. This will draw out some of the heat from the inflammation. Polyethylene bags are excellent for this as long as you don't put the paw into one but only wrap it around the wet compress. A puppy can run around on three legs perfectly well, so that if it has a broken paw, the vet will put the leg in a splint to rest it, and the puppy will probably use only his other three legs. I know of one adult Labrador who only has three legs—one had to be amputated after a shooting accident—yet he is the perfect gundog and regularly goes hunting with his master.

Fresh Air. *I have read that puppies who do not get enough fresh air and sunshine get rickets. How on earth can I, in midwinter, give my Saluki puppy either of these commodities in any quantity?*

I think what you read was probably referring to kennel dogs being kept in dark, airless places. The average puppy who gets the usual amount of walking exercise, and who is given supplementary vitamins, is unlikely to suffer from rickets. I think it far more important to keep a young puppy warm than to open all the windows and give it fresh air, and possibly a chill.

As far as possible, puppies should be protected from sudden changes in living temperature; drafts can be fatal to puppies. Therefore, the kennel or basket in which a puppy sleeps should always be raised off the floor, away from any drafts.

If the dog is accompanying you in a car, see that the

window doesn't make a direct draft in his direction. Puppies should never be allowed to put their heads out of car windows; this can cause running eyes, which are often difficult to cure.

Garden Behavior. *How can I keep my new puppy off the flower beds? He is ruining my garden.*

There is only one way to teach your puppy not to destroy the garden, and that is to put wire netting temporarily around the flower beds and valuable shrubs, for puppies can completely wreck a flower bed in a few minutes of play. The words "No, naughty!" must be used in a thunderous tone if the puppy attempts to go into forbidden areas of the garden. Teach him basic obedience, and never leave him free and alone in the garden before he is properly trained—that is the golden rule for gardeners who own puppies.

Make sure the puppy never empties its bladder on your lawn. The urine of a bitch is fatal to lawns. First the urine appears to kill the grass, and then the grass grows back dark and green and coarse, which is most unsightly. Keep a rough patch of grass for the puppy's toilet and make him use it always.

The eating of earth and stones shows a mineral deficiency in puppies and should be treated by giving a mineral supplement or other suitable tonic. Never let a puppy play in a garden where there are rats. Rats are carriers of diseases fatal to puppies. If your garden becomes infested with rats, get in touch with your local public health office at once.

Gastritis. *What is gastritis?*

Gastritis is a very common illness in dogs. It is an inflammation of the mucous membrane of the stomach or of the whole stomach wall. Vomiting is usually the first sympton of this trouble, and a tremendous thirst. Diarrhea often accompanies these symptoms.

The most common cause is of a bacterial origin, but

gastritis can be caused by faulty feeding or by a puppy's eating unsuitable things. It is very difficult when a puppy is young to stop its eating everything it gets in its mouth.

The first symptom is usually the regurgitation of a meal, and the vomit is covered with a watery and slimy mucus, often tinged with yellow or green. Occasionally the vomit is bloodstained from the breaking of small blood vessels, due to the strain of vomiting. Should the vomit be dark brown and resemble coffee grains, the dog is extremely ill owing to internal bleeding, and no time must be lost in getting professional help.

In all cases of gastritis, a vet's help must be sought. Light food such as Sustagen, sips of egg white, and nutrient supplements are all excellent.

The puppy must be kept warm and comfortable. Any vomit must be wiped immediately from his mouth and coat or it will smell badly. Gastritis is often a forerunner of distemper and other serious diseases, so never try to treat it at home. As a first-aid measure, a bismuth mixture helps to soothe the inflamed mucous membrane. Your druggist will make it up for you.

Glands. *What ought I to know about swollen glands?*

I could fill a book writing about glands. As you probably already know, glands are the drains of the system. They drain poisons from the bloodstream and act as filters. It is for this reason that when a puppy has a sore throat, the glands in its neck get enlarged. They are draining off the poisons from the throat.

There are, in a puppy's body, two little glands at the base of the tail called anal glands, which can be a perfect nuisance. They contain fluid to lubricate the bowel movements. Sometimes, if the puppy's stool is very soft, these glands get overful and become painful. The puppy tries to ease the pain by dragging its bottom along the floor. Most people think this dragging is caused by worms; but nowa-

days, when most people have their puppies wormed regularly, this is not often the case. It is far more likely to be
enlarged anal glands.

A vet will squeeze a dog's anal glands manually. It is not
a painful procedure, but it may have to be done at regular
intervals. Actually, this condition usually occurs in older
dogs. I have never seen it in a young puppy.

When a puppy chases its tail, it is often one of the first
symptoms of anal gland trouble, although this occurs in
hysteria as well.

Grass-Eating. *My Corgi puppy of eleven months eats grass
all day. What is the matter with her? She has a reasonably
balanced diet.*

Your Corgi is probably bilious and wishes to get rid of
excess bile by eating grass; she will then be sick, and you
will see that the frothy fluid she brings up is tinged with
yellow. That is excess bile. Sometimes dogs will eat their
breakfast and then be sick, and the vomit is covered in froth
and bile, but once they have been sick, they may attempt to
eat the food again. Should the puppy eat grass continuously, a few days on a bismuth mixture, as for humans, soon
corrects this condition. Magnesium trisilicate mixture is also
excellent. Dosage is as for children. It is quite harmless.

Puppies these days do not get a chance to wander over
the countryside as they did in the old days, eating the kinds
of grass their systems sometimes need, so if your puppy
doesn't seem hungry, I should try taking it to the country
and see if it goes for grass. Dogs mostly relish the coarser
grasses.

Very often Nature knows best in matters of health, so
never try to force a puppy to eat when it doesn't want to. A
day's starvation often clears up whatever is annoying its
tummy, and the following day it will feel fine. A little
honey in its drink of milk has a cleansing action on the
stomach, besides being nourishing. Puppies, however careful

you are, do eat the most appalling rubbish every time your back is turned, so sometimes vomiting is a good thing.

Greed. *I was given a diet sheet by the breeder of my Cocker, but she gulps her food and could eat a lot more than I give her. What should I do?*

Cockers are often very greedy dogs and, if permitted, will eat until they are so fat they can hardly walk. Under no circumstances feed her more than the correct diet; once you have a puppy too fat, it is very difficult to slim it.

The diets I give in this book are adequate. If you reckon one-half ounce per pound of body weight (normal weight, not overweight), you will strike a happy medium.

Greedy dogs are always easier to train than pernickity ones, for with tidbits you can win their attention and devotion! Little pieces of apple are useful for training a puppy; most of them like apple, though some prefer raw carrot. These can do no harm.

Grooming. *Is it really necessary to groom a short-coated dog? My puppy, a Chihuahua, has such a thin coat that I think brushing would hurt him.*

Grooming is not absolutely necessary with a short-coated puppy that lives in the house, but the massaging effect that grooming has is beneficial to the skin: it helps circulation and removes dirt and dandruff. One needn't have a stiff brush, which might scratch your puppy; a baby's hairbrush is just as good. Finish off with an old piece of silk.

When the puppy comes in from a muddy walk, let it get dry and then brush the dried mud off. If you have an old towel, dry the puppy as much as possible with that, and keep it very warm until quite dry. This is where a hair drier comes in useful—a few minutes under that and the puppy is dry.

Long-haired puppies should have a brush and a comb in

their toilet equipment. The hair should always be brushed against the coat in the first place. This not only gets out tangles but it also stimulates the pores of the skin and removes any dead and broken hairs.

Most puppies like being groomed. Any sign of temper must be firmly stopped, right from the start; hold the puppy by a short lead on its choke chain and, if it snarls, tighten the choke chain until it feels uncomfortable; loosen immediately it stops growling. Encourage it with kind words all the time it is being groomed, and praise it a lot when you have finished. Your attitude toward this operation counts a lot, as does the gentle way you groom it. One must realize that tangles hurt in dogs just as much as in humans.

If the hair is very matted, dampen it before attempting to get the tangles out. This helps enormously. (See "Brushing.")

Growling. *My puppy, a Corgi, growls in a most menacing way when I try to pick her up or get something she is playing with from her. Should I slap her nose?*

Under no circumstances slap your Corgi's nose. This is a cruel and quite ineffective practice. It makes a puppy worse, not better. If you ever have to smack a puppy, do it with the palm of your hand over its hindquarters. I find, however, that a good shake and a thunderous voice are far more effective. Some Corgis do growl badly, and they must be made to give up what they are playing with directly you ask for it. The way to make a puppy do this is to keep a choke chain on; then, when you want to take something away and the puppy growls, just suspend the puppy until it gasps for breath, at which point the object you want will fall out of its mouth. Immediately praise the puppy and kiss it, if you do kiss your puppy. A tremendous show of affection is absolutely necessary.

Growling, curiously enough, is not always a sign of bad temper; sometimes it is purely and simply "talking." My own Dane puppy often growls when her tail is wagging furiously and I am scratching her chest. It is a sort of series of grunts of happiness. To anyone who didn't know her, she would appear to be growling menacingly.

A puppy often growls because it is overtired and wants to be left alone. All puppies should have ample rest. Any sign of growling should be a warning to the owner to put the puppy into its indoor kennel or basket and let it sleep. After all, what other sign can a puppy give to show that it has had enough of something?

Guarding. *At what age should a puppy guard the house?*

It is impossible to fix an age for the development of the guarding instinct in a puppy. Some puppies mature very late, but if my own Dane puppy is a guide, she barked at strangers coming to the house at four months. That didn't mean, however, that she would have guarded the house. Had a burglar entered, I have no doubt she would have run away. It takes time for a dog to learn who may come to the door and enter and who may not. It is far better to have a friendly puppy than a nasty-tempered one.

Undoubtedly, training helps to teach a puppy to guard. In my case, I had another little dog who is an excellent guard and, when she barked, the puppy naturally picked it up. I taught my puppy at three months to attack on command, even in the face of gunfire. But I don't recommend this for inexperienced handlers.

I think if the average puppy learns to bark by a year old, that is what most people can expect. I think all puppies should learn to greet people with a wagging tail on the command "Talk," even if they have been barking at their approach. The word "Cease" must be brought into use at a very early age, for, make no mistake, once you have a yapping dog, you will find it very difficult to make it stop.

If your puppy truly loves you, the guarding instinct comes naturally. It is only dogs who have no deep affection for their owners that prefer to be friends with all and sundry. Give your puppy as much time as you can in your company, talk to it, play with it, and teach it new things to do all the time—it will then guard you naturally.

Gums. *The gums of my German Shepherd puppy are very inflamed, and she keeps brushing one side of her face with her paw. What is the cause?*

This is probably due to teething. She may possibly have a permanent tooth coming down before the temporary one has fallen out. This causes inflammation, and the puppy should be taken to a vet to have the temporary tooth taken out. If this is not the cause, there may possibly be a piece of meat or other food impacted underneath the gum. Take a matchstick and flatten one end with a penknife; wrap a tiny piece of cotton around the end, and gently probe around the tooth where the inflamed gum is, to see if there is anything foreign there.

The gums may get inflamed naturally in the course of teething, and there is nothing much one can do, except give large bones to help the puppy get rid of the unwanted teeth.

If, however, the puppy is over six months old and has its permanent set of teeth, there may be an abscess under the tooth, and veterinary advice must be taken. The cure will probably be antibiotics.

The gums should be watched to see that a growth of gum doesn't begin to grow over the tooth. This sometimes happens where there has been a foreign body in the gum. If this occurs, it will have to be cut off by a vet, using a local anesthetic.

Gun Training. *I have a lovely Golden Labrador puppy of five months old. My husband would like to shoot with it. Where do I get it trained for gun work, or can we do this at home? We are both inexperienced with dogs and have only just come to the country from a town.*

Labradors make excellent gundogs; the basic training for all work, whether it be gun, criminal, or film work, or just ordinary good behavior, comes with patient insistence on simple exercises like the "Wait, Sit, Down, Heel, and On" commands. Unless a Labrador is steady when the gun is fired, it will probably rush in and get shot. Therefore, before you even attempt to teach it to seek for game, or to retrieve game or rabbits, you must teach it to walk to heel off the lead and to stay standing or sitting when you are standing still.

The retrieve is taught with an old rabbit skin, rolled up. The puppy must never be allowed to chew it, but must bring it to hand at once, raising its head for the handler to take the skin or bird from its mouth when it is fully trained.

There are a number of gundog societies. You can write for the name and address of one in your area to the American Kennel Club, 51 Madison Avenue, New York, New York 10010. If you wish to train your puppy yourself, join one of these societies and get expert advice and help. Otherwise put an advertisement in a hunting publication for a keeper to take your puppy and train it for you. You will find ads in *Field and Stream*, for instance, for gundog training, or you can place a classified ad stating your needs. Trainers won't take puppies under six months old. I think having your puppy trained by an expert is the best method, although it means losing the companionship and love of your puppy for some time.

Hair. *How often do puppies molt? My crossbred Collie of eleven months is covering everything with hair.*

Puppies usually molt twice a year, with the exception of Poodles, who don't molt—they have to be clipped. You should brush your puppy at least once a day with a wire brush to get all the loose hairs out. A bath often works wonders in getting a lot of the hair ready for combing or brushing. In summer some people clip their Collies, which get such heavy coats; that is, of course, if it is only a pet dog and not wanted for show.

Handling for Show. *I want to show my Boxer, but he is wild and uncontrollable. What can I do?*

Get a good book on training, or attend a training class. Some training schools and clubs have special classes for show handling, when experts in the show game tell you what to do. If this sort of class doesn't exist in your neighborhood, I suggest that you have my book, *Dog Training My Way* (Stein and Day, 1972). Mr. and Mrs. Prince, owners of a Great Pyrenees dog, supreme champion at Crufts 1970, were trained by me, which proves obedience training helps show dogs.

In the meantime, train your puppy to walk to heel on a loose lead and to stand quite still on the command "Stand." Get him accustomed to having his mouth opened and his teeth examined by strangers. His gait is most important. You must hold the lead so that he has plenty of room to run freely without galloping. The first time you are asked to move him will be for the walk, the next time for the trot.

With Boxers it is very important to get them to really extend themselves to show their gait. If the puppy leaps about or jumps up, a judge cannot see this gait properly. Don't keep fiddling with the puppy in the ring; let him rest when the judge is not looking your way. Never let him be a nuisance to other puppies just because you want your puppy to look alert. Take a toy or tidbit into the ring with you to get his interest at the crucial moment. You are not allowed to have someone outside the ring to attract the puppy's attention. If you can, stand away from him while he is being appraised by the judge; it helps the judge enormously, and he will appreciate your good training. Do not get into conversation with the judge; this is not allowed. Only answer the questions he asks you.

The preparation of a puppy for show is an expert's job,

or it can be learned over the years. The nails must be filed short. The puppy's coat must be presented in first-class condition. His teeth must be scaled if they are at all brown. He must show fitness and alertness without being scatty. All these things help even a puppy with faults to show itself at its best. Clipping and trimming can make a vast difference in a puppy. Many faults can be hidden by expert trimming, so never try to do this at home; it is worth spending a few dollars to get an expert to do it.

Try to arrive at the show in plenty of time. See that the puppy isn't molested by people in the show who want to pet him. They may be carrying germs. They will certainly tire him out. Be ready for your class when it is called. Try to relax yourself. Don't be too downhearted if you don't win at first. Remember, every judge has his own ideas of what he wants—the next one you show under may give you a first. Never say catty things about other people's dogs—it doesn't pay.

Hard Pad. *What is hard pad? How can I protect my puppy from getting it?*

Hard pad is a disease that we knew nothing about twenty years ago. Now, with modern vaccines, the terror has been taken out of it. The symptoms of hard pad are similar to those met with in distemper—dullness, hot nose, rising temperature, and shivering. It is essential to call your vet in the early stages or paralysis may occur.

Hard pad is the forerunner of meningitis, fits, etc., and eventually the pads of the dog become hard. It is from this that the disease got its name.

Nowadays you should have your puppy vaccinated when it is nine weeks old. It is at this age that the immunity to disease the puppy got from its mother at birth is lost. No puppy should be taken into public places, towns, or parks without being vaccinated first. The vet will vaccinate your puppy and give you a certificate to show that it has been done. Booster doses at intervals during the dog's life should always be carried out. There is a special booster dose that lasts ten days, and many people give this to their dogs before attending a big dog show, where disease is always present.

People must not imagine that because their dog is vaccinated, it cannot get hard pad. It can, although if it does catch it, the attack will be much milder and more easily cured than if it were not inoculated. It is well worth the cost. There is nothing so heartbreaking as to have reared a puppy and then to lose it with hard pad. It is a killer disease and needs expert advice and nursing. The convalescence is slow.

Heart Trouble. *My puppy's heartbeats at four months old are 170 per minute. Surely this is very fast?*

You do not say what breed this puppy is, but for any breed this pulse rate is far too fast and suggests congenital heart disease. The heartbeats of a puppy that has rested for about five minutes should be around 70 per minute. If your puppy shows no signs of distress and can run about without panting excessively, I shouldn't worry too much. Ask your vet to check whether his heart is unsound; if it isn't, I should forget the heartbeats. Only if the puppy faints or shows signs of distress on exertion would I begin to worry.

Uneven heartbeats are far more to worry about than a fast pulse rate. There are plenty of drugs available to the veterinary profession for the treatment of heart troubles, but if a puppy has a bad heart, I doubt if it is worth keeping.

Heat. *When will my puppy first come in heat?*

Eight to ten months is the usual time, but some don't come in heat until a year. There is no fixed time, so don't worry if your puppy is late. It lasts from seventeen to twenty-one days. If it doesn't go after twenty-one days, consult your vet.

The bitch is ready for mating from about the eighth to fifteenth day. Before that, dogs don't pay much attention to her. Some bitches are highly irregular so it is never safe to go by this. Chlorophyll pills given every four hours do much to protect your bitch from unwelcome attentions from dogs. It doesn't matter how many you give a bitch; these pills are hamless. You can increase the dosage if dogs still pay her unwelcome attention.

Heel Work. *How do I teach my dog to walk to heel on the lead? She is a Labrador aged ten months and terribly strong.*

You should have trained this puppy months ago; now you will really have to jerk her hard on a choke chain. You should have a four-foot-long leather lead with a safety clip, and when she forges ahead, jerk her back firmly to behind your knee and praise her. Always give the command, "Heel," prefaced by her name. Don't be afraid to jerk her really hard. In between jerks, keep your two hands together over your own tummy—that will stop her jumping up. The lead should always be held very loosely. A tight lead means that you will never stop the dog pulling.

Hepatitis. *My friend's Corgi has just died of hepatitis. What is this disease?*

Infectious hepatitis is caused by a virus and was formerly known as Rhubarth's disease. This is a disease that in its mild form is very often passed over as indigestion or a chill, and for this reason the infected dog can infect a lot of other dogs before the disease is diagnosed. Hepatitis can kill a puppy overnight.

It is, of course, a jaundice, with the usual high temperature, prodigious thirst, sickness, and pain in the tummy. At a later stage, the yellow tinge typifying jaundice will be noticed on the mucous membranes of the eyes, mouth, etc., and in the vomit. This disease is usually fatal.

The most sensible thing to do is to have your puppy protected against hepatitis at the same time as the hard pad and distemper vaccinations. Your vet would tell you all about these inoculations.

Be sure not to give the puppy any yolk of egg to eat, but the white and a little honey are excellent. It must be kept extremely warm and given clear water to drink. If you can get it to take some Sustagen or other fortified milk substitute, which is a complete food in itself, you will be conserving its strength and not overburdening its stomach. A vet must be consulted at once, if you are to have any hope of saving the puppy's life.

Hiccups. *Every time my Dane puppy eats, it gets terrible hiccups. What can I do for it?*

This is very common in puppies. They bolt their food and get this spasm of the diaphragm. There is nothing to worry about, it will pass off. The puppy should grow out of it in time. As you can't make a puppy hold its breath, the only thing you can do is to give it a drink. Personally I would do nothing.

Hormones. *My ten-month-old puppy doesn't lift his leg yet. Is there something wrong with him?*

The lifting of the leg in male dogs denotes sexual maturity. Some puppies mature later than others. They usually lift their legs between ten and twelve months old, but it doesn't denote that there is anything wrong if it doesn't occur for some time after that.

When a puppy is castrated, he goes back to squatting like a bitch, even if he has learned to lift his leg before the operation. Sometimes people grumble that castration doesn't work because the puppy continues to lift his leg.

This is not the case. It all depends on how long the puppy has had full use of his glands before the operation. They store up a sufficient quantity of hormones for some considerable time. That is why a puppy should be castrated round about six to eight months old to get the early benefit from it. (See "Castration.")

House-Training. *How do I house-train my puppy?*

The house-training of a puppy is the first and most important training it has to undergo. I believe in really giving up about two weeks to this important function. No one, however good they are with dogs, can house-train a puppy without some mistakes occurring. Therefore, in my opinion, it is best to take up any valuable carpet so that if the puppy does puddle, the carpet will not be ruined. The urine of a bitch can take the color out in a few minutes; that of a male puppy is not quite so drastic. Ashe Laboratories of Guildford, England,* make a preparation that stops the color coming out if it is applied quickly enough. The trouble is that one doesn't always see a puppy puddling somewhere, and the damage is done before one can do anything. If I were getting a new puppy, I would buy a bottle of this preparation and keep it handy. Then I would take up the living-room carpet, leaving the underfelt for warmth, and would ignore remarks like "What will our friends think?" All sensible people will sympathize with your wish to train the puppy quickly and properly.

Regularity is of the utmost importance in quick house-training. You have to take the puppy out to its allotted spot at least twenty times a day. Always use the same spot; then the scent will give the puppy the right idea. Always use the same encouraging words like "Be Quick," which can later be shortened to "Quickie." It can be very useful to have your

*Look for similar American products advertised in the dog magazines.

puppy trained to puddle on command. Regularity is essential if you are to teach the puppy to defecate when you wish it to. Most puppies at six weeks will want to move their bowels at least four times a day. This part of the training is usually easier than the urine side of it.

The main thing to remember is that puppies naturally pass urine immediately they wake up, after food, and when cold, frightened, or excited. Therefore, if you want a clean puppy, try to take it out before it wakes in the early morning. Assist this by darkening the room it sleeps in with curtains. It is easy to pop the puppy out after its food because you should watch it feed anyway, in case it chokes. Never creep up behind it without talking to it, or you will find the shock makes it puddle inadvertently. Keeping it warm in winter is of vital importance, especially at night. The use of an infrared lamp or heater, if your house is not well heated, helps enormously.

Never smack a small puppy for making a mistake; it has no control of its functions at all when very young. Show it what it has done, scold it by voice alone, and put it out; that is all that need ever be done. When I say show it what it has done, I don't mean rub its nose in it. I merely mean take it near enough to the mistake and say, "Naughty dog," in a low voice.

If you have an indoor kennel, after you have played with the puppy, take it out, and then put it back in its kennel. If you never allow it to roam the house for the first week and you take it out at least twenty times a day, you will progress very fast, for the penny soon drops, and once the puppy understands what you want, it will try to oblige. If you have a dirty or wetting puppy after three months, your training is at fault.

Mothers with a young family always at their heels find it extremely difficult to watch a puppy closely enough to get it clean quickly. People at business during the day also have trouble. Always buy a young puppy in the summer if possible; then, if you are busy, you can put it in a playpen in the garden. The sun will do it good and if it does puddle, it doesn't matter. What does matter is your attitude to its mistakes in the house. You must never be a lazy person who lies abed in the early morning if you want a puppy to be clean. Dash down in your nightclothes, if necessary, if you hear the puppy whining. You will be surprised how quickly a puppy learns to whine when it wants to go out.

People often ask me at what age a puppy scratches at the door to go out. Some puppies never do. Highly intelligent ones do so at about three months. But if one has a way with dogs, one picks up its ideas by telepathy. I had my Dane puppy clean night and day by ten weeks.

Hunting. *My Beagle puppy spends its whole life with its nose on the ground hunting something or other. I cannot train it. What should I do?*

Your Beagle puppy is only doing what Nature intended it to do. If you must buy a hunting dog for domestic purposes, you must expect this sort of thing. The only way to cure it is to train it so well that its thoughts are more on you and on your commands than on interesting hunting scents. It will take a strong-minded person to have this effect on a Beagle.

Beagles should be trained from eight weeks old, and the training should continue until at least twelve months old. If the puppy runs away, when out walking, it must be kept on a long line and jerked back to you with the words, "Come here." The main thing is to try to give it some natural hunting by taking it for long walks in the woods. Do not call it until you actually wish to put it on the lead. If you call it continuously, it will get bored with you—Beagles are not very interested in human beings, anyway. I think they make unsuitable household pets.

Hysterectomy. *I own a Spaniel bitch puppy, but living in a flat in London, I cannot cope with its coming "in heat." Can you advise me what to do?*

If you cannot cope with a bitch in heat, the only safe way to end this trouble is spaying, or hysterectomy as it is known in the human world.

This should be done at about six months old, as it becomes more dangerous as the bitch gets older. There is always a risk attached to this major operation, but if you get a good vet to operate, this is not too great a chance to take. The bitch will be kept at the vet's for about three days. There will hardly be a scar on her side, and there should be no ill effects afterward.

You have to be very careful to diet a spayed bitch; they tend to become lethargic and fat if you give in to their pleadings for food.

Hysteria. *What causes hysteria?*

Hysteria can be caused by worms or by inbreeding or by hard pad and distemper, or even by a foreign body in the ear. In this case, the dog rushes around in circles and gets so giddy that it falls on the floor and foams at the mouth from exhaustion.

A puppy should be wormed twice before it is three months old and then once more at six months, after which you should always keep a careful lookout for worms in its stool. If none are seen, however, and unless the puppy has other symptoms, worms should not be present. Sometimes after an attack of hard pad a dog gets meningitis, which then causes fits.

Puppies do sometimes get hysteria when fed on white bread, due to the agenizing of the bread and the consequent lack of vitamin B. But if you are giving your puppy vitamin B, as in Vionate, then it is unlikely to get hysteria from this cause.

The treatment of the puppy is to apply cooked compresses to its head and to keep it from hurting itself while in a hysterical fit. Keep it quiet in a dark place until fully recovered. Hysteria often goes off completely when the puppy has finished teething. If the hysteria continues, consult your vet.

Indigestion. *My puppy has horrible bad breath. Is this due to indigestion?*

Bad breath may be due to a number of causes—worms, indigestion, bad teeth, or the aftermath of distemper or hard pad. You will have to eliminate each cause in turn. The same indigestion mixtures as humans use are a first-aid remedy—bismuth, milk of magnesia, etc.

Be sure the puppy isn't very constipated. If it is, liquid medicinal paraffin is a good remedy and can be bought at any drugstore.

If this bad breath continues, consult your vet, as it is unusual in puppies. This condition is usually met with in old dogs whose gums have receded, giving rise to pyorrhea. (See "Breath.")

Infection. *I want to take my eight-week-old puppy shopping with me every morning. Do you think it will catch something if I do?*

I should think it highly likely your puppy will catch some infection if you take it shopping at such an early age. Towns are hotbeds of infection. Urine is the carrier of most diseases, and although an adult dog may show no signs of being ill, it still can be a carrier. Never let your small puppy talk to an adult dog for this reason. People always want to pet puppies, but they may have petted a dog that was carrying something and they will pass it through their hands on to your puppy.

Not only is there a grave risk of infection in towns, but

no puppy should be asked to walk at that age, unless you are willing to carry it most of the time. This is another reason for leaving it at home. I think four months is early enough to take a puppy shopping. By that time his inoculations will have had time to give him some immunity.

Never let anyone come to your house who has a sick dog at home. Never put a puppy in boarding kennels if you can possibly help it and, if possible, ask the vet to call at your home to give it the inoculations. In my opinion, surgeries can also be a source of infection.

Infrared Lamp. *I am getting a new puppy next week. Our house is awfully cold as we heat by electricity and only have the heating in the rooms we are using. How can I keep the puppy warm at nights without its costing the earth to have an electric fire on?*

The best way to deal with this problem is to have an infrared lamp. It should be hung from the ceiling somewhere cozy for the puppy. He will snuggle under it and judge for himself how near he wishes to be. In winter, most breeders these days put infrared lamps in their kennels. A warm puppy is always a quiet puppy at night. It is the cold ones who shriek and wet their kennels. Perhaps you could make the puppy an indoor kennel and warm it with an infrared lamp? This is the ideal thing and not at all difficult to carry out if you are handy.

Don't get an infrared lamp mixed up with an ultra violet lamp, which is for sun-ray treatment and would burn a puppy badly. The infrared lamps use about 450 watts and are thus very economical.

Never take a puppy up to bed with you, thinking, "Poor little thing." A habit once started is almost impossible to end without a battle. Battles aren't good for the puppy or the owner. The kitchen is the best place to keep a puppy, where puddling on the floor can be easily mopped up.

Inhalations. *My eleven-month-old Spaniel has got bronchitis. Would it help her if I could make her inhale friar's balsam?*

Yes, undoubtedly it would help her, if she could be made to do it without scalding herself or you. Most young dogs would be very frightened by this, I think. But perhaps she is a trusting puppy and knows you are only helping her. The basin you use for friar's balsam (tincture of benzoin compound) will be useless ever after for anything else, so use an old one that you can throw away. It also stains terribly.

If your puppy has a blocked nose, a little Vicks Vaporizing ointment on the end of your little finger inserted up its nostrils would help clear the blocked nasal passage. Be sure to wipe the nose clean so it can't lick any of it.

Injuries. *I have an older dog and a new Great Pyrenees puppy. The Great Pyrenees has very sharp dewclaws, which got caught in the older dog's collar when they were playing together. The dewclaw got torn badly. What should I have done to prevent it?*

There is nothing you can do to prevent it except keep the nails on the dewclaws very short. If these dewclaws weren't a show standard of this breed, I should suggest having them surgically removed; they are the cause of a lot of trouble. If your puppy is only a pet, and you have no intention of showing it, I should get the damaged dewclaw removed, especially if it is on the front leg.

My puppy has swallowed half a crown.* Will it pass through all right?

It is highly probable that there will be no complications following the swallowing of your half a crown. Watch the

*A half-crown is a heavy coin about 1¼ inch in diameter.

puppy's stool for two days. If it doesn't come through, then consult your vet. If the puppy seems unable to breathe properly or is in pain, consult your vet at once. It may have inhaled the money, but I think this most unlikely with such a big coin.

My Gordon Setter has cut his leg on some rusty barbed-wire. Will he get blood poisoning?

Blood poisoning is a very old-fashioned word. Nowadays antibiotics have cut the risk of any wound going septic. But what you must do, after cleaning the wound and getting some antibiotic dressing for it from your vet, is to ask him to give the puppy an antitetanus injection. Any wound that is deep and dirty, such as a barbed-wire injury, should always have the protection of an antitetanus toxin.

Inoculations. *People have warned me that if I have my dog inoculated against distemper or other diseases I may, in fact, give him these diseases. Is this true?*

All vaccines are made from the bacteria or viruses of the disease, but they are either given in a dead form or so weak that the disease cannot be given to a puppy. What does happen is that in receiving these harmless doses, the puppy builds up an immunity to the disease in question by manufacturing antibodies. Therefore you can quite safely have your puppy protected against disease by having it vaccinated at nine weeks old and by giving it booster doses at intervals of two years or according to your vet's advice.

If you are going to a big show with a puppy, it is safer to give a specially made ten-day protection dose, which gives immunity for this length of time. This, of course, is in addition to the ordinary vaccine you had given to the puppy at nine weeks. No puppy may be shown until the age of six months.

Be sure to have the inoculation given to the puppy in the flank. A lot of dogs have given their first bite when being done in the shoulder. Hold the puppy under your arm so that it can't even see the vet giving the injection from behind your arm. You should try to get your puppy to be friendly with the vet, so that its pulse doesn't race with fright when he comes.

Inoculations should be given when the puppy is in good health.

Insurance. *How do I set about insuring my puppy against accidents and diseases?*

Many types of canine coverage—for veterinary fees resulting from accident or illness, expenses for recovering a lost puppy, or death from any cause—are available, though your regular insurance agent or company may not handle them. There are agents who specialize in canine insurance, and insurance companies that offer this kind of coverage. The American Kennel Club, 51 Madison Avenue, New York, New York 10010, will mail you a listing.

You should, of course, carry liability insurance in case your dog bites someone or otherwise causes injury or damage.

Jaundice. *My brother tells me he has had his puppy inoculated against jaundice. Can you tell me a little about this disease?*

Jaundice can be present in the puppy from several causes. There may be something blocking the bile duct, preventing the bile's escaping from the liver into the small intestine in the usual way; it has to be absorbed, therefore, by the lymphatics, and some of its constituents are then deposited in the body, causing the well-known yellow appearance of the mucous membranes, etc. This blockage may be caused by a gallstone, or a swelling in the lining of the intestine such as occurs in acute constipation, which prevents the outflow into the bowel. There may be many other causes such as T.B., tumors, cysts, etc., but few are likely to be met with in a puppy. The most likely cause of jaundice in a puppy is the virus of contagious hepatitis. The temperature rises to an alarming degree and the puppy becomes very ill. Unless veterinary aid is sought quickly, the puppy may die. The urine often becomes green, and the stool clay-colored and offensive. Vomiting is often present, as well as convulsions or fits.

The treatment of jaundice must, of course, depend on the cause and symptoms present. If the cause is obstruction, an enema is sometimes given to relieve the constipation. An operation may be necessary, but if it is contagious hepatitis, antibiotics will be used. In all cases of jaundice, expert advice must be taken without delay.

Jaw. *My Golden Retriever of ten months got its jaw stuck open the other day and seemed in agonies for about a minute. What had she done?*

She had obviously dislocated her jawbone. Puppies do this sometimes. Sometimes pulling gently on the bottom jaw will make it slip back into place. If you cannot help the puppy, take it to the vet, who will probably X-ray it and put it right under an anesthetic.

My puppy has an undershot jaw. What does this mean?

The word "undershot" simply means that the teeth of the bottom jaw are in advance of those of the upper jaw; in an overshot jaw the upper teeth protrude above the bottom ones. These faults are mostly hereditary and will be penalized in the show ring. The bite should be absolutely level in the perfect puppy, just meeting in the center. But many puppies have the upper ones very slightly overlapping. This would not be penalized to any great extent if the puppy were perfect otherwise. All these points have to be taken in perspective.

Joints. *My Dane puppy has enormous joints on its front legs. Are they rickets?*

If you are giving mineral-vitamin supplements in your Dane puppy's meals, these enlarged joints are unlikely to be rickets. All big dogs should have "knobby knees," although the front leg joints are actually not knees but are equivalent to wrists in the human being. The bumps and lumps on the joints straighten out as the puppy matures, as do the limbs, which turn slightly outward in a large breed. Turning inward or being pigeon-toed is not so easy to correct. Do not give heavy puppies too much exercise, or the legs and shoulders will be wrong. The elbows turn outward in an overheavy dog. Once the damage has been done in puppyhood, nothing can be done in later life to correct it.

Jumping. *My children will keep making our crossbred puppy jump for a ball. Will this make it bow-legged?*

I have never heard of a puppy being made bow-legged unless it was a very very heavy one like a Bull Mastiff or St. Bernard, and these breeds of puppies aren't at all interested in jumping for a ball. I very much doubt if it will hurt your mongrel; they are usually very tough.

Some people try to teach their puppies to jump high jumps and long jumps, in preparation for obedience trials, which include jumping. No puppy under about eight months should attempt to do these things. For one thing, if it bumped its legs badly, this might eventually lead to cancer of the bone and, for another, such jumping is too much of a strain on a growing dog. But, by all means, teach it to jump little obstacles.

I do know that jumping can hurt a puppy's back sometimes, especially Dachshunds with their extra-long spines. Occasionally a dog will jump for a ball and displace a disk. The best first-aid remedy for that is to catch hold of the puppy by the tail, if it is a small one, or by its hindquarters if a large one, and suspend it upside down for a minute. This extends the spine, and often the disk will slip in again.

Kennel. *Do you think it is better to keep my puppy outside in a kennel until it is house-trained? We have a very small home.*

I don't like keeping puppies outside, especially in winter, when it is very difficult to keep them warm. I prefer to make an indoor kennel and keep my puppy in some quiet room where it can rest when tired.

My husband made my last indoor kennel out of plywood and wire netting. It was made for my Dane puppy of six weeks old and measured 2 1/2 feet square. The frame was made of wood 1 1/2 inches square. The sides were filled in with plywood. The back was half open, the open part being covered in 1/2-inch mesh wire netting and the other half was solid plywood. The front had a wire netting door, the other half being again solid plywood.

The open back was placed against a radiator, thus the puppy could not burn herself, but was kept very warm at night. She slept on an old cot mattress one end and newspaper for about two weeks and then became quite clean by eight weeks old at night. I am sure an indoor kennel hastens house-training.

One can make an indoor kennel out of an orange box by making a large hole in the division and putting solid wood on one end and a netting door on the other. In all cases, the indoor kennel should stand on another orange box or some device to keep the puppy off the ground away from drafts.

Kennel Club. *I wish to show my puppy. What is the procedure?*

The Kennel Club is the ruler of the show world. You have to register your puppy there first of all. You will want to begin with small local shows. The Kennel Club will supply you with a list of its member clubs, so that you can find a club in your locality or a breed club that interests you. When you decide on a show, get the entry form from the show secretary, fill in all the particulars asked for from your registration certificate, and send the entry form with the appropriate money to the secretary of the show concerned.

The address of The American Kennel Club is 51 Madison Avenue, New York, New York, 10010.

The American Kennel Club is always willing to answer people's questions in relation to pedigree dogs and their showing. There is a monthly magazine called *Pure-Bred Dogs—American Kennel Gazette*, in which are published transfers of dogs, and other interesting matters concerned with shows and showing, etc.

Kidneys. *Do you think my puppy has a chill on the kidneys? She is ten weeks old and puddles every ten minutes.*

I think it most unlikely that your puppy has a chill. If you are giving her a lot of milk or other fluids to drink, she probably will puddle every few minutes. It sometimes seems that fluid goes in one end and out the other in perpetual motion. Until the puppy has learned to control her bladder, you simply have to watch her and put her out as soon as she starts sniffing around or looking at the door. Puppies don't ask to go out until they are three or four months old. Until that time you just have to develop second sight.

You will, of course, have had your puppy inoculated against leptospira canicola, which is a kidney disease that often proves fatal. The vet will give an inoculation that covers this and leptospira icterohemorrhagic infections. Both these diseases are fatal to young puppies. They are urinary infections. Never let your puppy sniff at lampposts or she may pick up these infections. A puppy infected by these diseases will be very ill with a very high temperature.

Barley water can be given to drink; it has a soothing effect on the kidneys. In Argentina all kidney trouble is treated by the natives with "Barba de Maiz," which is the brown hairlike stuff you pull off the corn cob. This, infused in boiling water and drunk soon cures kidney trouble. If your vet fails to help your puppy with kidney trouble, you can always try it, now that corn on the cob can be bought.

Leads. *What type of lead should I have on my Poodle for training purposes? Leather ones seem so heavy.*

I don't think it matters what type of lead you have as long as it isn't a chain one. This would cut your hand when carrying out the exercises. In my school I use 1/2-inch bridle leather leads 4 feet long with a safety Trojan hook. This type cannot open up with jerking as can a scissor type. The ordinary spring hooks can come off the lead when jerked and cut your hand.

Nylon collars and leads with these safety hooks are very suitable for Poodles, and they are washable. You cannot, by the way, train a Poodle wearing a Poodle collar. You should have the correct choke chain, and an ordinary leather or nylon collar not thicker than 3/4 inch. You must have a choke chain because a leather collar when jerked would ride up and hurt the puppy's ears.

The lead should be held in the right hand when a puppy is being trained on your left side and must be held loosely. Any tightness on the lead causes a dog to pull.

Leather leads that get wet should be rubbed over with saddle soap, allowed to dry, and then polished with a soft rag. This preserves the lead. The hooks should have oil in the spring parts at least once a month. Never hold the lead over your wrist by the loop. If you happen to fall, you might get dragged by the dog.

Leave. *How can I make my Saluki leave other dogs alone? He wants to play with them all and has twice been bitten.*

The only way to make him "leave" is to jerk him really hard on the choke chain when approaching another dog, giving the command "Leave." If one minute you let him play with other dogs, and the next minute try to make him leave them alone, you are asking for trouble in the early stages of his life. Always be consistent with puppies. If you say "Leave," you must really mean it and punish the puppy if he doesn't obey you.

Unfortunately there are so many unaccompanied dogs that run free and annoy your puppy that discipline under these circumstances is very difficult.

Leptospirosis. *What is leptospirosis?*

There are two forms of leptospirosis, both of which seem to be most frequently spread by contact with lampposts, hydrants, and the corners of buildings, where dogs urinate. It is always wise to prevent your puppy from the very start from sniffing at these things.

The first kind of leptospirosis is called leptospira ictero-hemorrhagica, which is jaundice (see "Jaundice"); the other is leptospira canicola, which is related to the other form but which affects the kidneys. Many dogs can be carriers of this disease without actually being visibly affected. The usual symptoms of this illness include fever, diarrhea, and pain over the kidney region. The mucous membranes become pale, and the breath is horrid. Veterinary attention is a must if the puppy is to make an uneventful recovery. Nowadays, using a vaccine against this disease has reduced the horror of it.

Lice. *My Scottie puppy never stops biting and nibbling itself. What is wrong with it?*

I think if the puppy is very young, it may have lice. Many kennel dogs bring these pests to their new home with them. The trouble is that the nits hatch out after you have cured the first infestation, so that you have to continue to treat the puppy for some weeks.

Gammexane powder in the form sold for dogs at druggists' usually cures this trouble, but if the puppy is old enough to bathe, I would bathe it in a pesticidal soap, leaving the soap in when you dry the puppy. Repeat every three days for ten days—that should put an end to the trouble. Sometimes excessive meat will cause overheated blood so that the puppy bites and scratches continuously. Therefore watch his diet, and reduce the protein if the washing or powdering does not stop it biting itself. Lice can be picked up from other dogs, or from chickens in the fields. Sporting dogs can get lice from the game they retrieve. Hedgehogs are full of fleas but not so often lice.

Licking. *My puppy will lick my baby. Does it matter?*

Yes, I think it does matter. I consider any licking of the face unhygienic and even dangerous. Puppies carry the eggs from a worm infestation on their tongues and mouths from licking themselves, and these could be transmitted to your baby, causing a serious complaint of the muscles, which could, years later, cripple the child. Always be sure to have your puppy thoroughly wormed before admitting it to the family circle.

Also, be sure to wash your puppy's face and mouth at least once a day. Remember, they eat their food with much splashing and they are not like cats, who clean themselves with their paws; they can't clean more than can be reached by the tongue.

Provided your puppy is wormed and washed, an occasional lick for the baby will do no harm at all. Whatever happens, don't let your baby pick up your anxiety. There is nothing so pathetic as a child who is afraid of puppies.

Lights and Liver. *I have an Irish Wolfhound puppy; he eats*

*me out of house and home. Could I feed him partly on
lights as they are cheap?*

You can feed a puppy on anything that comes from a
steer or sheep, but you won't get the same results by
feeding lights as you will if you feed him on steak or shin of
beef.

If you feed liver in excess, you will give the puppy
diarrhea, but it has a high vitamin-A content, which is of
great value to puppies. I find one of the cheapest foods for a
big puppy is canned meat-and-liver dogfood, plus biscuits or
brown bread. My own Great Dane Juno was fed on a
relatively lean canned meat and did very well. A large puppy
of ten months needs one large and one small can per day,
plus biscuits according to condition and appetite.

When puppies are under three months old, they must
have raw beef, as the protein is not so high in canned meat.
I think half raw and half canned reduces the cost considerably. All large puppies need at least 1 1/2 pints of fresh milk
a day. This milk should be reduced to one pint per day at
six months old. I never think it pays to save money while
rearing a big puppy. Once he is adult, you can feed him on
the cheaper meats without doing so much harm.

Limping. *My puppy, a St. Bernard, is limping. As she is
only ten months old, it can't be rheumatism surely? I can't
see anything wrong anywhere.*

Puppies can have rheumatism if kept on damp or drafty
floors. But with a large puppy like a St. Bernard, I think it is
far more likely to be rickets. These puppies grow at such an
enormous rate that few owners realize what a lot of vitamins and minerals they need for proper growth. Often these
puppies are cow-hocked, and any excessive exercise lames
them. They only need what exercise they can get playing on
their own in a garden or field, for about fifteen minutes,
twice a day.

If everything like rickets and rheumatism has been explored, examine your puppy's feet. There may be a bleb coming between the toes (see "Blebs"). The pads may be sore. People who keep these puppies on concrete-floored kennels cause them to get sore pads. If this has happened, harden the pads by bathing twice a day in methylated spirits—that is, providing there is no bleeding part. If there is actually a sore on the pad, this must be healed first and protected by a boot to cover the entire paw. Never bandage just the paw; the puppy will get it off. Bandage the pastern and the whole of the paw, otherwise you are inclined to get severe edema (swelling), which will be most painful to the puppy, and he will tear the bandage off.

Loose Bowels. *My puppy always seems to have rather loose bowels. What is the cause? He seems lively enough.*

There can be so many causes of loose bowels, it is hard to pinpoint any particular cause. If the color is normal, either brown or deepish yellow, it is not likely to be very loose; if the puppy appears well, a soft stool usually means that it is having too much fat, too much food, or has a chill.

The first thing to do is to cut his food slightly. The next is to give nonfatty foods, and the third to make sure he has no temperature. If all this is done in one day and the stools after two more days are still loose, I should consult a vet. He may have worms, jaundice developing, or gastroenteritis. Some very excitable puppies will always have loose bowels. The act of getting excited seems to have this effect on the bowel. Very nervous dogs are affected in the same way.

Feed the puppy on drier food, cut the quantity of milk, take the cream off the milk. Never give the yolk of egg, only the white. Never give horse meat. If you give canned meat, choose one that has a very low fat content. Bones will constipate a puppy, so give him more bones to chew. Chewing bones helps the digestive juices to work, which aids digestion. A bismuth mixture from the druggist will help to stop diarrhea if that is what your puppy has. Keep him very warm at night.

Love and Laughter. *I came to one of your training classes the other day and noticed how you were always hugging the dogs and laughing with them. Do dogs like this? I am not that sort of person.*

Being inhibited is one of the greatest drawbacks I know of to happy and speedy training. Most people cannot let their hair down and really get down to the level of a dog's mind. I have so often noticed the expectant look on a dog's face when I am having a game with him. I am just another dog in his eyes. That is what you should aim to be—a superior dog. So many people don't truly love their dogs enough to do this. You cannot change your own character. With a puppy, especially, you have to be very gay when training it, for it will get bored. A bored puppy looks listless and almost ill. It is too tired to do anything well. A quick lesson in a bright cheery atmosphere, insisting on instant obedience and then giving unstinted praise, is the answer for an unenthusiastic puppy.

Some people think it unhygienic and nasty to kiss a puppy; if this is so, I must be riddled with germs as I have kissed thousands of dogs in my lifetime. But I always do it behind their ears with their faces cupped in my hands. A sweet-smelling puppy is a delight to kiss.

Lying Down. *I am over fifty years old, and my new puppy is driving me mad. She never stops rushing about every evening, expecting me or my husband to play with her. How can I teach her to lie down quietly?*

This, I am afraid, takes time. You must put her to the sit and then lift one front paw while pushing the opposite shoulder. This will make the puppy lose her balance and lie down without fuss. Then you must hold up one finger and say "Stay!" in a thunderous voice. If she gets up, put her down again, and, if necessary, again and again, getting crosser each time until she realizes you are going to win. When she stays for a few seconds walk a few yards away, with your finger up and a soothing tone of voice occasionally saying "Good girl, stay." If she stays for a short time, go back to her and praise her and romp about. By this method she will learn that to stay means a good romp afterward. When she is used to doing the exercise with you present, teach her to do it with you out of sight, and eventually when you put her in another room. That is the answer to being pestered in the evening. Having cleared your conscience during the day by giving her plenty of exercise, insist that she give you peace when you need it.

Some puppies never rest, and if the owner cannot teach the above exercise, the only thing to do is to get the largest marrow bone you can find and give her that to gnaw all the evening. Why must she be free at all? Surely by evening all young puppies and children should be in bed. Put her in an indoor kennel or in her basket in the kitchen, and your query need never have arisen.

Magnesium. *Is magnesia good for my puppy?*

Magnesium in various forms is used quite a lot with puppies. There is nothing safer for a stomach upset than milk of magnesia, giving anything from a teaspoonful to a tiny dog to two tablespoonfuls to a large one.

It is an antidote to lead poisoning. A saturated solution is often used for enlarged joints. Magnesium sulfate is used to draw the sepsis out of injuries; in fact, in some form or other, the puppy is almost bound to meet it. Sometimes puppies have hiccups or gas very badly. A teaspoonful of magnesia will quickly relieve these complaints.

Mange. *I have a puppy with follicular mange. I am terrified* *my children will catch it. Yet it is such a sweet little thing, I don't want to put it to sleep. What can I do about it?*

There is no need to worry about this—it is not contagious. It is passed to a puppy in the bloodstream of the mother, and can easily be cured by bathing it in a pesticidal soap and leaving the soap in. Sarcoptic mange, on the other hand, is very contagious. Bright red irritation is present, and the skin, where the hair has come off, is greasy and inflamed. The vet should be called at once to deal with it, the dog's bedding should be burned, and the premises it uses disinfected. If the puppy bites itself too much, it may have to wear a large circular collar to prevent its getting its head round to do so. Most vets keep one of these for patients. Your children should not come in contact with the puppy. In fact, if you can get the vet to take it and cure it for you, it is an excellent way out of a difficult situation. For however careful one is, a mangy puppy somehow manages to get near the baby!

Mange is caused by tiny mites that you can only see under the microscope; they look perfectly horrid, with suckers on some of their legs. Mange usually starts on the muzzle, working backward toward the tail. Never wash a dog in carbolic as some people tell you to do. Dogs absorb it through the skin and can die from it. Treat mange only under expert supervision.

Mating. *At what age can I breed my bitch puppy? She has just come in heat for the first time.*

You mustn't breed her until the second time of coming in heat. She is not adult enough to bear the strain of a litter at eight months old.

Bitches shouldn't be bred unless you wish them to. Never allow it just for the sake of the health of the bitch. It has long ago been proved that there is more risk of disease in a bitch that has bred than in one that hasn't. Neither dog nor bitch is ever quite the same when they have bred. Besides spoiling a bitch's figure, it makes them less affectionate, I think.

No male dog should be used for stud purposes until at least twelve months old. Stud dogs are inclined to fight, so unless you really wish him to be used for this purpose, don't let him "have a bitch" in the mistaken idea you are being kind. When you keep him as a pet, he will be a nuisance once he has been allowed to mate.

Meals. *How many meals would you give a six-week-old Pom?*

A Pom is no different from any other puppy. They all need five meals a day at six weeks. I think 6:30, 10:30, 2:30, and 6:30 should be the main meals and then last thing at night a warm drink of milk. If a puppy is noisy at night, it often pays to give one of the heavy meals at night, which includes meat, cereal, and milk. The milk can be changed to a fortified milk substitute, which is of course a complete food.

No puppy should run about after a meal. It should rest after having been taken out for toilet purposes. It is most important to see that the puppy digests its meals in peace. Don't allow children to interfere with it or play with it for at least an hour.

Always remember, a puppy will eat until it is nearly ready to burst. Never increase the food beyond the correct amount in the mistaken idea that it is still a hungry "poor little thing." If you overfeed a puppy, the food will only pass out of the body as urine or feces. Its body cannot absorb more than a certain amount. Excess food gives rise to flatulence and distension, both of which are uncomfortable for the puppy and unpleasant for the people it lives with. Distension can be dangerous and can actually kill a puppy.

No puppy can grow bigger than it is genetically designed

to be; more food won't make it grow any bigger. Too little food, on the other hand, can stunt it.

Regularity of meals is of the utmost importance, because the puppy's saliva begins to flow at that time. In this saliva are the enzymes and other factors that help to break down the proteins and fats in the body. Even rattling its feeding bowl will make a puppy's saliva flow. Association of ideas is of paramount importance in the dog world. So if you are an unpunctual person, you must change now where your puppy is concerned.

The meals should roughly consist of two-thirds protein and one-third carbohydrates in the form of meat and bread or biscuits. Milk should always be given, and added minerals and vitamins are of vital importance to a growing puppy. No puppy should be fed at the mealtimes of its owner, or it may start begging at meals. There is nothing so annoying as having a dog watch every mouthful that goes in your own mouth. He sits there with a dejected expression, and one feels a brute if one doesn't share the meal with him. The result of sharing a meal is that the puppy's tummy gets upset, for it never knows when to expect food. The puppy probably gets too fat with having more than its rightful diet, and altogether it is a bad thing for both puppy and owner.

Meat. *Please tell me whether canned meat has the same food value as, say, shin of beef, and whether horse meat is good for puppies. I have never had a puppy before and don't know whose advice to follow.*

Naturally the breed of dog makes a vast difference in mapping out a diet. But horse meat is definitely far too high in fat content to be good for puppies. I had one canned dog food analyzed, and it was found to have 3% fat compared to shin of beef 3.6%, and 12% protein, compared to shin of beef 23%, which shows that canned food is better for puppies than raw meat as far as fat content is concerned, for few puppies tolerate fat well. But for large puppies growing into big dogs, the canned meat would be of less value in protein than the shin of beef. Therefore one could choose a happy medium by feeding half canned meat and half shin. This would equalize fat and protein, and the puppy should thrive.

Most canned meat has abundant vitamins added to its contents. If you use raw butcher's meat, you must add plenty of vitamins and minerals.

Milk. *How soon can I stop giving my puppy milk?*

If you are sensible, you will continue giving her some milk all the days of her life. Milk is a natural food and gives dogs lovely coats. What I don't approve of is giving dogs tea. Tannin is not good for them.

You do not say how old your puppy is, but until six months old a large dog should be having a pint of milk per day. This provides much-needed calcium, fat, and protein, besides minerals and vitamins.

Goat's milk is too rich for puppies—it should have the cream taken off it. Jersey and Guernsey milk is also rich and might better be given to a puppy in skimmed form. Few puppies thrive on too much fat. Milk should be given fresh, not boiled.

Some puppies as they grow up seem to refuse milk. If this is the case, make it into a little custard with cornstarch or an egg, and they will usually take as much as you want them to have. I have mixed milk with a little of the red gravy from the Sunday joint, and they have wolfed it.

I very often think animals know what is best for them, and you may find the puppy has some allergy or idiosyncrasy that means milk doesn't suit it after a certain age. Nowadays one can give artificially all the calcium and vitamins needed, so it isn't of all that much importance. As long as a puppy is thriving, don't fuss too much over its diet. If a puppy won't eat, starve it for a day; in the wild state dogs often don't eat for days on end. Animals benefit from an occasional fast.

Monorchids and Cryptorchids. *My male puppy doesn't lift his leg, and he looks as if he has only one testicle. Is this possible?*

Yes, this is possible, but until the puppy is adult, you wouldn't be wise to conclude that it is a monorchid. Some puppies mature sexually very late. Some never have either testicle descended; they are then termed cryptorchids. There is nothing that can be done about this trouble. Cryptorchid puppies may become bad-tempered and unreliable. But this temper doesn't often show itself until they are adult. As soon as the puppy has both testicles descended, he should start to lift his leg at about six months old. When a dog is castrated, he squats like a bitch. If, however, the dog had been entire for many years, this may not occur and he may lift his leg for the rest of his life.

You cannot show a monorchid or cryptorchid except in obedience trials. There have been many disputes in show circles whether a particular dog does or does not come under these categories. At shows where veterinary examination is required, the vet is supposed to check everyone's dog for this disability.

Dogs can breed if they are monorchids, and this disability is often hereditary.

Mounting legs. *My bitch puppy mounts my legs like a male dog. Is she wrong sexually?*

No, I don't think so. Many puppies seem to go through a stage of being neither male nor female and do behave like this. I would worry far more if a male puppy was doing it as it might mean he was going to be oversexed. There is nothing more hateful than owning an oversexed dog. They lift their legs in the house over everything and mount the children's legs or even cushions. I strongly advise anyone with a puppy like this to have it castrated at six months old or as soon as castration becomes possible.

I wouldn't allow your bitch to behave as she does; I would push her down sharply and scold her. Puppies don't seem to know what to do with themselves; they are always trying out everything. A good big marrow bone to chew works wonders with an overexuberant puppy.

Mouths. *What particular care should I give my puppy's mouth?*

All puppies should have their mouths examined regularly to make sure their teeth are coming through correctly. If extra teeth appear, they should be removed by the vet. If the gums get inflamed, a mouthwash should be used; or if the inflammation doesn't respond to simple measures, then the dog should receive an antibiotic.

It is most unlikely with a healthy puppy that its mouth will smell, but after distemper or hard pad the teeth get very discolored, and sometimes cause bad breath. Chlorophyll given internally will help this considerably. As the health of the puppy gets better, so will this trouble. Chlorophyll can be given ad infinitum without any harmful effect. The mouth—outside, not inside—should be washed every evening after the puppy's last meal; just use flannel with warm water and a little toilet soap to wash around its muzzle, and dry well with a soft towel. Dogs should always be hygienically kept; they seem to take pride in it. A dirty puppy doesn't seem to mind being dirtier; a clean puppy likes to be kept clean always.

Mucus. *My Great Pyrenees puppy has mucus in both eyes every morning, and the bottom lid looks inflamed. He is not in a draft. What is the matter with him?*

Sometimes these mild infections come with the puppy

from the kennels. If bathing with boracic lotion or Optrex doesn't cure it, a vet can prescribe an antibiotic and anti-inflammatory agent that should help your puppy's eye. Bulging lower lids can be most unsightly and become chronic if left without expert attention. Only a vet can really diagnose what is wrong. Eyes run when the puppy has distemper and other infections. But when that infection clears up, the puppy's eyes will recover. Mucus from the nose is, of course, a sign of ill health. A puppy's nose should be damp but not covered with mucus.

Nails. *Puppies' nails should be kept short, I am told. How do I cut them?*

The cutting of a puppy's nails is really an expert's job. The breeder usually cuts them short before selling you the puppy, but if they are long, take him to a dog-groomer or to a vet. Both these people should be able to do it and show you what to do in future.

Exercising a puppy on the pavements should keep the nails down. Only if the puppy never gets this road work should they need cutting; under those circumstances I have known them to need cutting every three weeks or so. It is best done with proper nail clippers. Cut only the curved-over piece that protrudes beyond the thick part which contains the quick. If you look at the nail from underneath it you will see that the end is almost transparent. That is the part to trim off. Cut the nail to within 1/6 inch of the end of the quick—this allows sufficient protection. The paw should be held firmly and the nail cut straight across. You can then file the roughened tips with an emery board file. If by any chance you do cut the quick, wrap the whole nail up in a piece of adhesive bandage, and it will soon grow out again.

Some puppies are very frightened when you attempt to manicure them, and you will have to have help. Never give in to them. Bathing, manicuring, and grooming are three things they just have to learn to accept.

Nasal Catarrh. *My puppy's nose is always running, but she seems well otherwise. What can I do for her?*

It sounds as if she has got nasal catarrh; perhaps she had a cold that didn't quite clear up, and that has left the mucous membrane of the nasal passages swollen. I find that a little Vicks Vaporizing ointment on the tip of the little finger, pressed up each nostril, clears the passages very quickly. Be sure to wipe off all excess.

Always treat all nasal conditions as infectious until proved otherwise. Keep the puppy warm and away from other puppies. Wipe her nose clean with cotton dipped in boracic lotion or witch hazel. Apply a little Vaseline to the outside of the nostrils to stop them getting sore. If this doesn't work, a little hydrocortisone is very soothing and anti-inflammatory. Usually fresh air and good food clear up this sort of condition very quickly in a young puppy.

Neurosis. *Some puppies are hopelessly neurotic. What causes a puppy to become like this?*

I don't believe that puppies are so neurotic; I think it is the way they are handled. Pernickity pups who won't eat this and that just need starving until they become hungry. If they think that looking at their food and turning away will make the owner immediately go and find something tastier to tempt them, they will do it again and again. This "neurosis" is unlikely to occur in a very young puppy. It is usually not very evident until about ten months old. By that time the puppy has learned how to "play up" its owner. Some puppies get hold of a piece of rag or some such article and refuse to give it up. They nurse it as if it were a puppy and show their teeth if the owner tries to get it away. This is a form of neurosis: in bitches it is an overdeveloped maternal instinct. They usually take the object of their fancy to their bed with them, and sleep with it under their chins just as if they were nursing a puppy. Sometimes bitches have to be spayed and dogs castrated if they behave like this because obviously there is something wrong with their sex glands. The trouble is that spaying a bitch has some risk attached to it. And if a male has an undescended testicle, he cannot be castrated. If this is the case, there is nothing to do but persevere with training.

Nerves. *My Poodle is a mass of nerves. I have tried coaxing him, but he will not walk in town. I am ashamed of him. What should I do with him?*

This is what happens to dogs when they become a popular breed; it is not your fault that he is so nervous. Don't sympathize with him. Don't stop in town to encourage him. Just carry straight on regardless. If he tries to sit down, jerk him on quickly—that is if he has a thick-linked choke chain. People will think you are very cruel, but pay no attention to them. By being firm and not giving in to his fears, you are helping him to get over them. Ask people to touch him if they will; if he shrinks away and attempts to bite, muzzle him and still ask people to touch him. While they do so, you must speak to him in a bold voice saying "Talk," "Good boy." Never let people hold out their hands for him to sniff; I know of nothing more likely to make a puppy nervous than that. They should go straight up to him and pat him firmly. An obedience class would help him to mix with other dogs, especially if the trainer will handle him for short spells at a time.

You can get the vet to give him sedatives, but as their effect is so temporary, I fail to see what permanent use they are at all. It is much better to be firm with him and cure him. I cure hundreds of nervous dogs in a year by the same sort of handling and, without exception, they love me after their training.

I reckon a nervous dog has either to be cured or put to

sleep; it is no pleasure owning one in this state. Nor can it be a happy life for the dog.

When a puppy is nervous within hearing of gunfire or bangs, get a toy gun and fire it often. He will soon take no notice of it.

Some puppies are shy of men and not of women. That can only be cured by asking men to take the puppy out for walks; if he enjoys himself, he will soon get over his nerves. Don't bother about toy Poodles shivering; they often do this purely from nerves. As they get braver, it stops.

Nightmares. *Sometimes when sleeping, my puppy yelps and cries as if in pain; she draws her legs up and down. Do you think she has a stomachache?*

I think your puppy is dreaming. When puppies dream, they may whine in a high-pitched tone and gather up their legs as if galloping. They only do this when in a deep sleep. Sometimes they are quite difficult to wake. There is of course no harm in a puppy's dreaming; you need do nothing about it.

Nose. *My dog's nose varies between hot and cold, yet she seems quite well. Need I worry over this?*

The answer is yes and no. A dry, hot nose is one of the first symptoms of serious illness, yet a puppy very often has a dry nose when it wakes up, especially if its accommodation is a bit too warm. If, after the puppy has been given a drink and taken for a short walk, the nose becomes damp and cold again, there is nothing to worry about. The dog sweats through its nose, and after some diseases like hard pad, the nose never completely recovers its nice moist look; it remains dry although it is cold.

The nose should be free from mucus whether thick or clear in consistency. If the mucus from the nose is thick and sticky, the dog either has a very bad cold or is sickening for a serious illness. Keep it warm and call the vet.

A dog's nose is of vital importance to it. All its enjoyment seems to radiate from its sense of smell. It can pick up scents a great distance away, and these convey pleasure, fear, excitement, or terror. A puppy in particular is governed by its senses, and smell means a lot to it.

Should a dog's nose bleed, make the dog lie down and apply a cold compress to its head behind the ears; it may be due to getting overheated or to a blow on the head. Or, quite simply, it may be the aftermath of a bad cold. If it bleeds copiously, call the vet quickly.

Nourishment. *I am just getting my German Shepherd puppy over hard pad. It doesn't seem hungry at all. How can I get it to take nourishment?*

Little and often is the answer. Try Sustagen (or some other fortified milk food), the white of an egg, or milk with a little honey. Sometimes baby rusks tempt it, and ice cream may tickle its fancy. A little beef broth or chicken soup is excellent. You can make veal jelly by boiling the veal bones until the juice sets into a jelly when cold.

Some puppies like pieces of apple or orange. These are good for them in small quantities.

The yolk of an egg should seldom be used; it is too fatty for a sick puppy.

I have known dogs to eat homemade sponge cake when they wouldn't touch anything else.

Nursing. *I know nothing about dogs, but would like to feel prepared if my new puppy becomes ill. Can you give me some hints on nursing?*

Nursing a puppy is very like nursing a sick child. The conditions in most homes can be adapted so that the sick puppy has what it most needs: warmth, cleanliness, peace and quiet, plenty of clean water, strict attention to diet, and medicines as prescribed by the vet in attendance.

If you have more than one dog in the home, the sick one

should be strictly isolated until all risk of passing on infection has passed. The food should be as advised by the vet. Dishes the sick puppy eats from should be absolutely spotless. The utensils that come in contact with it should be boiled once a day. The person looking after the sick puppy should be most careful to wash his hands after seeing to it. If possible, keep overalls or something old you can wear when seeing to the puppy. If the puppy is the only dog in the house, things are not so difficult.

Many owners are so terribly worried over the puppy's illness that they keep rushing in to see how it is. This is bad for any sick animal. The puppy needs to sleep and conserve its energy. If you have an indoor kennel for it, that is where it should be. The kennel should be in a warm place right out of drafts.

Another thing inexperienced people tend to do is to tempt the puppy all day long with food when it doesn't want it—they imagine it will die of starvation otherwise. An ill dog is best left without solid food for a couple of days; a light diet of milk and perhaps Pablum or Sustagen is best. As it recovers, it can be placed back on to scraped meat in small quantities.

It is most unwise to listen to well-meaning friends as to the cures they gave their dogs with the same symptoms; so many diseases have similar symptoms but are treated differently. Eggs, for example, would be unsafe for dogs with jaundice (only the whites should be given), yet in other diseases an egg is probably the most digestible food.

Try not to handle a sick puppy too much; naturally your love for it must be shown, but picking it up tires it. Should it be frightened of the vet, your reassurance is very necessary. It is funny that so many dogs are frightened of the vet though he has never hurt them. I suppose it is the smell of antiseptics he carries about with him.

A sick puppy should be able to lie stretched out in rest. Make sure his basket or kennel is big enough to allow this.

Dogs pick up fear very easily, and I have known sensitive ones to become worse when the owner has been terribly worried about them. Try and be cheerful when dealing with sick puppies; it gives them reassurance. I am perfectly certain animals worry over themselves if the owner worries. Remember, too, that you can often carry germs on your clothes; therefore, never handle anyone else's dog if you have a sick puppy at home.

One of the most difficult things to arrange is for a puppy to go outside to perform his toilet in winter, yet a house-trained puppy won't do it indoors. You must somehow fix up somewhere with a windbreak for it and be sure to put a coat on it before taking it out. Should it have diarrhea, newspapers are the best thing to use in a kennel; they can be burned.

Remember, carbolic is death to dogs, so never disinfect anything with that. The puppy might chew something that has been washed with carbolic.

Always be punctual in giving medicines. If a dose is once every four hours, it should be given dead on time. One cannot gad around, coming home late, and still nurse a sick puppy.

Always take away any food that the puppy refuses to eat, and throw it away; fresh food each mealtime is most important. Liver is the most tempting dish for sick puppies; they adore it. But it gives a puppy diarrhea if given in too great a quantity. If a puppy has pneumonia, a pneumonia jacket should be made for it out of surgical wadding (see "Pneumonia"). It should wear this for the whole duration of the pneumonia.

Occasionally when some ointment has to be applied to some irritating skin infection, the puppy may have to be muzzled to prevent its licking the ointment. Don't fret that the muzzle is cruel; a well-fitting one hasn't the slightest bad effect on the puppy after the first shock of it is over. The main thing to remember is that you are doing everything you can to cure it. It mustn't be handicapped in any way by oversentimentality.

Oats. *All the shepherds around us here in Scotland seem to feed their sheepdogs on porridge oats. Could I feed my Cocker Spaniel on them? It would save expense. I am an old-age pensioner.*

Yes, by all means, try out your Cocker on porridge oats. Provided they are well cooked and milk put over them, they would make an excellent meal once a day. Some puppies couldn't stand the amount of roughage in oats; it would give them diarrhea. But I think a Cocker would be all right.

The other meal you give your puppy should be one of meat in some form or other. Very tiny puppies should not have oats, but after four months old it should be quite safe—younger if the puppy is a strong breed.

Obesity. *My Labrador puppy is getting very fat. Will he grow out of it?*

Fatness comes only from overfeeding. This is extremely bad for any puppy. If you are the sort of owner who overfeeds, either because you don't know what diet to give or because you give in to every demand from the puppy for food, you are not likely to get your puppy's "vital statistics" right again very easily. Labradors should have about one pound of meat and one-half pound of biscuits a day when seven to eight months old, plus one-half pint of milk. If the puppy still stays fat on this, cut his biscuits. Dogs can live and be very healthy fed entirely on the protein diet of meat. It is only the fat and carbohydrates that cause a puppy to get fat.

Obesity is bad for the heart, puts a strain on the kidneys, and makes the puppy short of breath. Fat puppies usually suffer from gas and occasionally have unpleasant breath. They don't live as long as properly dieted dogs.

There is only one advantage in having a fairly plump puppy. If it does get ill, it has plenty of weight to lose before becoming skin and bone as it might do with distemper. But as sensible people mostly inoculate their dogs against distemper, this reason for having a fat puppy is not very valid.

Obligations of Ownership. *My neighbor is getting very rude about my puppy. She says he gets into her garden and digs it up. I go to work. How can I possibly stop it when I am not there?*

You sound as if you are one of the people who should not own a dog—not because you don't love him but because your way of life is unsuitable. If you have to leave your puppy free when you go to work so that he can annoy people and do damage, you must obviously be neglecting your duty to your dog and your neighbor. I have every sympathy with your neighbor. I think you should have a kennel made in the garden with a wire run attached to it. Exercise and feed your puppy before going to work, and then put it into its kennel. It should also sleep there; otherwise the change of temperature in winter might give it a cold. If it is kept cool, it will not suffer.

I should insure your dog against third-party claims. I feel sure if you apologize to your neighbor and assure her you are going to put an end to the nuisance you have caused, she will forgive you. Most people are fairly lenient where puppies are concerned.

Obstreperous Puppies. *My Boxer is a most obstreperous puppy. It knocks my front teeth nearly out, and the children go over like ninepins in his mad rushes. I do not want to squash him too much, but his behavior beats me at present. What can I do to make him more sensible?*

Most Boxers behave like this until they are fully trained

dogs. Not only that, but they become very independent if not disciplined. He must be taught to "wait" on command by putting him on a long string and tying it to something strong. Put him at the sit so that the string is completely loose, and call him. Before he has time to reach you, give the command "wait" and hold up your hand, all fingers outstretched. If he doesn't stop, give him the command again when he is nearing the end of the string, and the string will stop him; you must then go and scold him. Repeat until he stops in his tracks on the command "Wait"; then praise him. This training will only work if you have taught him to "come"; tidbits are permissible. If he won't come, you must use the string again, to pull him in to you this time. Give him some sharp jerks toward you coinciding with the word "come"; he will find it unpleasant not to come.

Now, when he dashes about your house, stop him with the word "wait," and you can then put him away where he can do no damage. This will soon teach him to behave. Jumping up must be stopped by a sharp slap on the nose as he jumps up. There is no other way except by hitting his nose with a wet rag. But how often does one have a wet rag in one's hand at that particular moment? Dogs hate being hit with a wet rag; it has a most sobering effect on them.

Obstruction. *My puppy nearly choked the other day. Luckily it coughed and seemed able to breathe again. I was very frightened. What should I have done?*

Naturally it depends on what is causing the obstruction. If it is some small object that has got lodged in the larynx, the best thing to do is to pick the dog up by its tail and hold it upside down. If this doesn't work, crook your little finger and try to fish up whatever is causing the obstruction.

Overfeeding can cause obstruction by the overfull tummy pressing on the diaphragm; this in turn sets up an accumulation of gas in the intestines, which can quickly kill a puppy. Occasionally pleurisy can cause obstruction and suffocation. Obstruction in the intestines can be caused by swallowing sharp pieces of bone, which can actually pierce the intestine. Only large marrow bones should be given to puppies to chew.

Worms can cause acute obstruction in the intestines. But sensible people worm their puppies at least twice before six months old, and more often if absolutely necessary. The stool of a puppy should always be observed for worms, especially segments of tapeworms.

If you think your puppy is choking from any cause whatsoever, call the vet. If it is suffering from gas formation in the bowel and the bowel is very distended, give it a small round of washing soda, which will make it sick and help greatly.

Oil of Sarsaparilla. *I have been advised by my neighbor to get oil of sarsaparilla to put on my eleven-month-old Peke, who is in heat, to keep the dogs away. Is this good?*

I think you would be better giving your dog chlorophyll by mouth and washing its backside with a solution made by dissolving one or two of the chlorophyll pills in warm water. The bitch is the troublesome one; she tries to flirt with the dogs and thus attracts their attention. Her smell will not attract them if she is properly medicated. It is never safe to trust any preparation for the last ten days of a bitch's heat. There may come along a dog so oversexed he can smell anything anywhere.

Be sure to wash the dog after the heat is over.

Pet Puppies. *The breeder who sold me my Corgi said it was sold as a pet only, and he wouldn't give me a pedigree. Is this fair?*

Breeders can make any restriction they like on the sale of a puppy. Obviously he thought the puppy would not be a credit to his kennel as a show dog. It is quite a common practice to sell a puppy on these terms. No warranty is attached to a sale of this kind; it is up to the purchaser to examine thoroughly what he is buying.

Pills. *How does one give vitamin pills to a puppy? Mine struggles and bites me when I try to put it down her throat.*

The best way to give any pill is to wrap it in a small piece of meat; most puppies eat meat hungrily, and the pills go down easily. I give my puppy a vitamin-mineral supplement that is in powdered form. It is unfortunately rather insoluble, but she doesn't mind, and eats it up easily with her morning Cornflakes and milk. I think if you start this habit with young puppies, they get accustomed to it.

All puppies should get accustomed from an early age to having their mouths opened without biting. Try opening the mouth and popping in a piece of liver, each time commanding the dog to "Open." I think you will find that your puppy will quickly learn to open her mouth on command, hoping for the liver.

You must never try to open a puppy's mouth with your hand on the bottom jaw. Always place your hand over the top of the muzzle, with your first finger and thumb in the puppy's mouth where the teeth are absent, just behind the large canine tooth when it comes through. Slight pressure on the roof of the mouth makes the puppy open at once. It cannot bite as there are no teeth there. Liquid medicine should be given at the side of the mouth by pulling outward the loose skin on the bottom jaw. This acts as a funnel. Keep the puppy's head up, and stroke its throat until you see it swallow. Always put the puppy to the sit before attempting any medication. Otherwise it might struggle and choke.

Plastic Toys. *My puppy adores my little daughter's plastic doll. Is it safe to let her play with it?*

No, I don't think it is safe without watching her. Plastic can so easily be eaten. Never give a puppy a plastic bag to play with. They can get their heads inside one and suffocate. Bones and large rags make quite suitable toys.

Poisoning. *The rat man came from the board of health the other day and laid down poisonous bait for rats. He said it wouldn't hurt poultry and the puppy, but I think my puppy has eaten some, and he is very sorry for himself. What can I do?*

Make him sick by putting a piece of common washing soda down his throat. After he is sick, give him a white of egg and call a vet. The vet will give you advice on the phone that you can be carrying out before he arrives.

Try and find out what the poison is. It cannot be very dangerous or you could sue the city. Why is your puppy outdoors alone? I think this most unwise in a young puppy. They eat everything, regardless of their safety. Puppies should be cared for like tiny babies, realizing that danger to them exists everywhere. (See also "Antidotes.")

Postmen. *I saw my eight-month-old German Shepherd have a nip at the postman's trousers the other day. Luckily the man never saw him. What can I do to stop this?*

First of all, take out an insurance that covers third-party risks, or you will be in trouble. The next thing to do is to keep your puppy in the house; don't let him have the run of the garden. If you take him for one reasonable walk per day and let him run free in the house or take him with you when you go shopping, that is all the exercise a puppy needs. When left to roam the garden by themselves, dogs inevitably grow scatty and tend to bite. There is nothing else for them to do. If possible, teach him to "talk" on command to people, so that he becomes friendly with everyone. German Shepherds develop the guarding instinct, which means they protect their owner if anyone goes near him. This is a most dangerous trait and must be checked from the very start. Try not to rush to the door when the postman comes or you will excite the dog. Biting people is partly nervous excitement and partly viciousness. Let the dog warn you with some barking when strangers come to the house, and then check him by making him lie down.

Potbelly. *My Weimaraner puppy seems potbellied. What am I doing wrong to make him like this?*

As you have not told me what you are feeding him or whether he has been successfully wormed, it is difficult to answer your query.

Generally speaking, potbelly is due to one of two things: worms or rickets. Turn the puppy upside down, and if his tummy has a blue tinge, then it is most likely worms. Sometimes one gets a great ball of worms from a potbellied puppy. Many owners worm their puppies but don't examine the feces to see if the puppy really has passed worms. If you are unsuccessful with your worming, send the puppy to the vet.

If the potbelly has come from rickets, you must quickly give vitamin D in the form of cod-liver oil—1 teaspoonful per day—or some supplement containing vitamins A and D. The puppy needs air and sunlight when possible. Sometimes puppies drink so much they blow themselves out. This must not be mixed up with potbelly. It will go down to normal as the puppy digests its meal.

Quarantine. *I am importing a puppy from the U.S.A. Can I visit it in quarantine? Which are the best quarantine kennels? People tell me the dogs are most unhappy without their accustomed warm blankets, etc., to sleep on. What happens to dogs that have been reared in the house?*

This quarantine problem is always a knotty one. I know of one boarding establishment that refuses even to give the pet Poodles a blanket or toy from their previous existence. Such places should never exist. Most of the kennels are run by people who care well for the dogs. I shall be pleased to recommend such kennels to people.

If a dog is fretting for the owner, a daily visit is ideal, for you can stay and play with your dog if you wish. If the kennels refuse this, take your dog away and send it elsewhere—it means the owners of such a place aren't dog lovers. I think there is a risk in kennels for dogs accustomed to a centrally heated home. But surely under those circumstances it would be better to import a puppy in the summer. If it is your own pet dog, you just have to take the risk. Some kennels are of course heated in winter. If you feel your dog would not thrive in quarantine, I fear the only alternative is putting it to sleep before you come to England. The girls who are in charge of the dogs in most kennels do try to make their charges happy. There is no way out of obeying the quarantine laws, so it is useless to write to me about it. Six months is the minimum safety period. Dogs have been known to get rabies after this time.

Quivering. *My little Poodle quivers all the time she is out with me. People say to me, "Oh, look at the poor little thing, she is cold." Is she cold or has she got St. Vitus' dance?*

I very much doubt that your puppy has either of these complaints. Puppies do of course quiver and shiver with cold; but they also quiver from nerves. My own little dog does it although she is not nervous. Italian greyhounds do it a lot, so do Poodles and other toy dogs. You have to learn to ignore it. As soon as the puppy is running free and is gay and happy, the quivering stops. There is no cure for it. It affects mostly the tiny breeds that have roach backs as part of their standard. They look even more miserable because they naturally put their tails between their legs.

Rat-borne Infections. *I live near a railway siding, and I see rats scampering about there sometimes. My neighbor lost her Setter from some disease of rats. What was it?*

Leptospirosis icterohemorrhagica is the disease you are talking about. I should get on to your local health department at once and ask them to abate the nuisance—the risk of rats' carrying disease to your dog is a real one. The disease is passed by the rats' urine, and no one can ever tell where that will be in your garden. Leave no food around to attract them. Take care that your puppy doesn't come in contact with any poison the council may use. A bite from a rat could be death to a small dog, so never go hunting rats, however much your puppy wants to do so. He can hunt squirrels or rabbits but not rats.

Refusal of Food. *My puppy takes from anyone anything in the way of food he is offered. Can I teach him not to do this?*

Yes, you can do this. But it is rather risky because, should he have to go into kennels at any time, he might refuse to take food from the stranger who looks after him. However, this is what you do to teach him.

Get someone to come up and offer him food; as he goes to take it, ask them to sweep their hand in front of the puppy's nose with a thunderous command "Leave." It must appear as if that person is going to smack the puppy's nose. Repeat this as often as the puppy goes to take the food. Usually on the fourth or fifth attempt, he realizes this is something unpleasant and turns his head away. Then he must be given the food by you and praised for all you are worth.

Rest. *My King Charles Spaniel is so fond of me that she follows me about the house all day long. I feel she shouldn't do this, but she whines if I shut her away. What should I do? She is six months old.*

All puppies should have adequate rest; that is why I recommend everyone with a young puppy to have an indoor kennel—somewhere the puppy can be put so that it is not disturbed. Puppies need peace and quiet if they are to sleep deeply and relax. Treat them just like a human baby in this respect. Pay no attention to any whining or barking; just steel yourself to ignore it. Then the puppy will give up. I reckon it takes about two days to do this. A puppy of about eight weeks should only play for about an hour three times a day. The rest of the time it should be quietly resting and growing.

Far too many owners play too much with their young puppies and wonder why they get bad-tempered. A tired puppy is a bad-tempered one who often bites its owner. This of course is in a vain attempt to show the owner that it has had enough. Don't scold it for this, but put it to bed for a rest.

Rheumatism. *Can you please help me? I think my Irish Wolfhound puppy has rheumatism. He used to jump up with his paws on my shoulder, but now refuses to do so as if he were in pain. Could he have rheumatism at nine months?*

I very much doubt that your puppy has rheumatism, unless you keep him in damp and drafty quarters. I think it far more likely he has hurt his sacroiliac joint and that it pains him to get into the position. I should try to lift his back quarters, leaving his front feet on the ground. This extends the spine and will often allow the displacement to return to its rightful place. If he shows extreme pain as you press his back gently, I should say he had a displaced disk or kidney trouble. Is he passing too much water? I should collect some and have it analyzed. Sometimes an infrared lamp will do a lot of good. It can be placed on the dog's back while he is resting in the evening. But remember, infrared should not feel hot to the hand, just nicely warm. The heat from these lamps warms the deep tissue.

I would definitely get expert advice.

The treatment of rheumatism these days with cortisone and other drugs has advanced so far that even if the puppy has got this complaint, there should be a good chance of its clearing up with professional advice.

Rhubarth's Disease. *What is Rhubarth's disease?*

This is infectious virus hepatitis, which I have dealt with under "Hepatitis." These liver and kidney diseases are so complicated that the ordinary owner gets muddled up. Have your puppy inoculated against this disease, and you can reasonably expect that your puppy will be safe from its ravages.

Rickets. *My seven-month-old St. Bernard puppy has bow legs. Will these straighten? I give him four pounds of meat per day.*

I suspect your St. Bernard has rickets. You are grossly overfeeding him, and the extra weight he must have put on has aided and abetted rickets. You should cut his meat to one and one half to two pounds per day, and give him multivitamin capsules containing all the vitamins needed for his health. The capsules should be given in his meat. Don't give him exercise or you are going to get his legs more bowed than ever. By now I expect his elbows are sticking out. What a pity you bought a big breed without taking precautions to see that it didn't develop rickets. With luck you may be able to cure the rickets or at any rate prevent them from getting worse. Calcium in the form of bones and by mouth is also highly essential.

Ringcraft. *I am taking my German Shepherd to her first show. Can you give me any tips on how to behave in the ring?*

The best thing to do is to watch the expert handlers and

as far as possible copy those who do well in your breed. Before going to the show, you will have to train your puppy to walk and trot quietly on a loose lead in a straight line, so that the judge can appraise her front and back action. A puppy that is jumping around all the time may be excused at its first show if very young, but no judge is going to put it to the top if he can't see it properly. Your puppy must get accustomed to having her teeth examined. Do not allow your puppy to annoy other exhibitors. Rest her when the judge is not looking your way. Then stand her correctly and try to leave her alone while she is being looked at. Have something she particularly likes in your hand, but train her to stand and "wait," or she will walk forward, spoiling her stance. Don't keep brushing her in the ring—it is bad manners. Many people "top and tail" their dogs, which means holding up the head and tail by hand. This, in my opinion, should be against all rules. If a dog can't show himself, he is not a show dog. However, until the Kennel Club really clamps down on this method of showing, you will probably do it too. Always be ready when the judge is ready for you. Lift your dog onto the table if requested to do so; then stand away so the judge can see the dog.

Dress yourself nicely for the show ring, but don't arrive in your latest Paris creation. Remember, the judge is looking at your puppy, not at you.

Never address the judge unless he asks you something. Do not gossip with the next exhibitor and miss the judge's directions to you.

When asked to run your puppy, run her as fast as you can to show her gait but not so fast that she breaks into a gallop. Place her as far as possible to show her good points and mask the bad ones. Experienced handling can sometimes put a dog on top that the judge might not otherwise have noticed.

If you lose, don't say horrid things about the other exhibitors or their dogs. Just take it as a game.

Ringworm. *My puppy, an Irish Terrier, has round bald patches on its head and neck, and now I see my child has one like it in her hair. Is this ringworm?*

It probably is ringworm. This is a highly contagious fungus disease that causes intense irritation and round, bald, reddish patches, which form crusts as the exudate dries. The puppy should be isolated immediately and treatment started under professional advice. Undoubtedly your doctor will deal with the child, and the vet your puppy, but I expect the treatment will be pretty much the same. Tremendous precautions must be taken to prevent spreading this disease to other dogs or other people. If your vet will take the puppy to cure it, I should let him have it. It is very difficult for a housewife to carry out all the treatment and hygiene necessary in these cases. Ringworm usually occurs in young animals like puppies in winter, so whether is is partly due to debility in the puppy and partly due to contagion, I do not know. It is the disease kennel owners fear second to the major virus infections.

Road Training. *I often see a mongrel down the road crossing the road, looking to see if traffic is coming before doing so. How have his owners taught him this? My Scottie would deliberately cross in front of a car if not on the lead.*

No one has taught the dog to cross the road. It is obviously a wanderer and has probably had one or two near misses. The intelligence of such a dog is quite high, and it has learned to keep out of the way of cars. It has probably been taken many times across the crossing where you see it and goes there by force of habit. You must teach your puppy to sit at the curb and wait until you give the command "Over." It should always be on the lead in a built-up area, however confident you are of its behavior. It is better to be safe than sorry. After years of this training a dog knows the drill and will then appear to have road sense.

No puppy has road sense. Guide dogs don't start their training until after nine months old, and it takes very experienced trainers to teach them. Even then they sometimes forget. I remember going for a walk with a blind lady and her guide dog, who was off duty without his harness, and he rushed across the road without stopping at all, very nearly causing an accident. Yet with his harness on, he was a model guide dog. That, I think, proves that association of ideas counts a lot with all puppies and adult dogs.

Road Work. *I am very keen to win a show with my Boxer puppy of ten months old. Everyone says he is a beauty. But he seems to have rabbit feet rather than the tight feet I have seen on other Boxers. What can I do to cure this?*

Steady exercise on the road is the very best thing for this. Make sure his pads do not get sore, especially if your roads have been recently tarred.

Half an hour a day at a steady walk or slow trot will soon get his feet right. If he will trot slowly beside a bicycle, that is the very best way of exercising him. Galloping about does little good.

The road exercise will keep his nails short, so very necessary in any show dog.

Rolling. *My Spaniel puppy rolls in things while out walking. I have scolded him, with no effect whatsoever. Why does he do it?*

This is an old pack custom. It was done by wild dogs to show the pack where they had gone. They would roll in a decomposed "kill." The only thing to do is to catch the dog and show him what he has rolled in and really scold him. My own Juno once did this and was so ashamed at her own smell that she went entirely on her own to the bathroom when she got home. She knew she always had to have a bath after rolling.

I know of no cure except training to cure this. You must keep awake when you are out walking and if you see the puppy sniffing very intently at something call him up quickly.

Roundworms. *I have just seen my Saluki puppy pass a great ball of wriggling round things in his stool. Are these worms?*

Yes, I should think so. They sound like ordinary roundworm. Every puppy is born with an infestation of these horrid creatures. But luckily their days are numbered as soon as you dose the puppy with a suitable worm cure. You can buy worm cures at a drugstore, pet shop, or stores where pet supplies are sold. Or your vet will give you a pill to put in the puppy's food. Nowadays there is no need to starve a puppy before worming. Simply pop the pill into his food. After about two hours the puppy will pass a stool with an abundance of dead worms. Should he not be clear after one dosing, he must be done again in two weeks.

Don't allow worm-infected puppies to lick children, or adults for that matter. The eggs are carried in the mouth of the puppy, and can be transmitted to man.

Selling Puppies. *I have a lovely litter of Sheltie puppies. This is the first time I have bred any. Is there anything I should know before selling them?*

The main thing is to have the puppies at least eight weeks old before parting with them. Younger puppies often get ill in inexperienced hands. Only when you have met as many ill-advised dog-owners as I have will you realize how incapable many of them are.

Never give an express warranty. This may get you into trouble. If you are asked, "Do you guarantee them show specimens, or healthy, etc.?" simply reply, "In my opinion they are." No one can take you to court over your opinion.

Always give the new purchaser a written-out diet sheet, and the pedigree and registration certificate. It is always wise to register the puppy in your name and then transfer it. If the puppy is over nine weeks old, have it vaccinated before selling it and hand the certificate to the purchaser.

Remind the new owner to keep the puppy warm on the way home. It has been accustomed to being with its brothers and sisters. I always wish breeders would charge a little more for their puppies and include a book on training with the purchase of the puppy. This action would save so much recrimination. Always worm the puppies before you sell them, and inform the purchasers of the date it was done. Never sell a runt; have it destroyed at birth. It never pays to rear rubbish. The vet will put it to sleep for you.

Beware of dealers coming round to buy your puppies *en bloc*. They sometimes get the most appalling treatment, ending up in pet shops or dying of cold. Make sure, as far as possible, that the people who buy the puppies are dog lovers and reasonably sensible.

Sensitivity. *My Poodle is so sensitive that if I scold her, she sits and trembles for the rest of the day. She is four months old. I cannot teach her anything when she is like this. Can you advise me what to do?*

Yes, get tough. This nonsense is a form of nerves that must be cured if you are going to have a sensible puppy. Make her do what you wish and praise her; she will soon get over her fear when you are firm.

Sickness. *My puppy has a delicate tummy. She throws up her food a lot. I have to mince everything for her. She is a Bloodhound. Is there any medicine I can give her to help her?*

I don't think one should fly to medicines for this sort of thing. It is curable by changing her diet to more frequent and smaller meals. People think big breeds have big tummies. They haven't. Give her five tiny meals, and I am sure your troubles will be over. Never feed her last thing at night.

Sit and Stay. *Every time I put my puppy to the sit, he gets up again. I have tried being cross. What do I do next?*

Push him to the sit more firmly, hold your finger up as you leave him and if he dares move, rush back like a thunderbolt and put him back where you left him. Only when you are very firm will he think it not worth the risk to move. Don't forget the love when he does stay. Constant practice is necessary for all these exercises. You also need patience and perseverance. The person who says, "My puppy won't do it," will never win. "My puppy will do it if I know how to teach him," is the right way to look at things.

Tail. *My Great Dane has a sore tail. She wags it against tables and things, and it will not heal. What can I do?*

I once had this trouble with my Great Dane, and I had a fiber-glass tail shield made to cover the wound. The wound was open to the air as I cut a hole for it in the shield. I kept it powdered with an antibiotic like sulfanilamide. It healed beautifully. The shield must be stuck firmly to the hair with zinc oxide plaster. The other kind of plaster comes off.

Teeth. *Is there any way of telling a puppy's age by its teeth as you can with horses and cattle?*

The answer to this query is, of course, yes, up to a certain age, but after the full set of permanent teeth have been acquired, it is only guesswork. A puppy is born with no teeth; between two and three weeks he gets his milk teeth, which are very sharp, and does not begin to lose these teeth until between three and five months old. At six months the permanent set of teeth should be complete. The changing of the teeth begins with the upper and lower incisors. It is amazing how quickly and unobtrusively a puppy loses its baby teeth and gains its permanent ones. Some people say they have seen baby teeth all over the place, but this has not been my experience. Occasionally a permanent tooth will come down before the baby tooth has fallen out. If it is loose, you may be able to give the baby tooth a little tug and it will come away easily. Otherwise, get your vet to pull it out for you.

It is most important to examine a puppy's mouth quite often during teething to make sure nothing like an abscess is forming or food is impacted where a baby tooth has fallen out. This examining of the mouth at frequent intervals is not only a safeguard against teething troubles, but a first-class way of accustoming the dog to having its mouth examined at shows later on, to taking medicines by mouth, and to having its teeth cleaned periodically. Frequent handling of a puppy's mouth makes it "soft-mouthed" so that it won't nip so hard when playing with its owner. Baby milk teeth can do a lot of damage to the owner's fingers and arms even though the puppy is only playing. As the dog grows old, the teeth deteriorate and become discolored if not properly cleaned and scaled. This cleaning and scaling should be done regularly throughout the dog's life. Your vet or dog's beauty parlor will do it for you. Few private owners are capable of carrying it out at home. The gums should be watched to see there is no overgrowth of gum caused by tartar on the teeth. If this "hanging down" of a piece of gum does occur, your vet will anesthetize it and cut the gum back. This does not occur in puppies, only in older dogs.

The age at which your puppy should first have his teeth cleaned cannot be forecast. Probably few dogs need this service until over the puppy stages. Bones help to clean the teeth and keep the gums healthy and free from pyorrhea. But the bones should be large marrow bones, not game bones or small bones of any sort.

Teeth Staining. *My Mastiff's teeth are horribly stained. She had distemper at six months old in spite of being inoculated. I have tried cleaning her teeth with toothpaste and it doesn't touch it. Is there anything else I could try?*

There is a powder called Vince that is excellent for removing stains from human teeth; you could try this. It is quite safe, and can be used as a mouthwash when a puppy is ill. A rag soaked in 10% volume hydrogen peroxide has a bleaching effect.

Training Schools. *I live in Kansas City. How can I find a training school near my home?*

If you write to The American Kennel Club, they will send you a list of training schools in your area. The address of The American Kennel Club is: 51 Madison Avenue, New York, New York 10010.

Uvula. *My puppy seemed to have a hoarse bark, so I opened her mouth, and her uvula looked swollen. What is wrong with her?*

It sounds as if she has tonsillitis. You should get in touch with your vet if she has a temperature over 102° F. Very often a sore throat is the commencement of a more serious disease. Usually the tonsils at the side of the back of the mouth are also swollen and inflamed.

Voice. *I live in a city apartment, and my Pekinese never stops barking. I am told there is an operation to stop him barking at all. Is it cruel?*

Most certainly not. I have had several dogs in my school whose owners had had them debarked. It is a tiny operation nicking the vocal cord as was done to all horses in World War I. The puppy can still make a very muffled noise and is perfectly happy. If the only alternative is putting him to sleep, I strongly advise you to have the operation done.

Wandering. *My Collie is a terrible wanderer. I let him out in the mornings and very often don't see him all day. Unless I chain him up all day, how can I keep him at home?*

Make home more attractive to him by training him, by keeping him with you whenever you are at home, by taking him for walks instead of letting him out on his own. You never know if he has caused an accident while out. I think you ought not to have a dog unless you become more responsible.

X Rays. *I think my puppy has a broken toe. I tried to push her foot under the shoe X ray in the local shop but couldn't see anything wrong. It is very swollen. Where can I take her to get an X ray done?*

I am concluding your local vet hasn't got one. If not, take her to a city where there is a large animal clinic or to a veterinary college. They have all equipment necessary for this.

Yawning. *My Saluki yawns all day long. Surely an eleven-month-old puppy can't be tired all the time.*

I suppose any puppy could be tired. But I doubt if this is the cause of the yawning. Is your home very hot? Puppies feel the heat a lot. Never let it near the fire. It may be liverish; if so, a tablespoonful of magnesia, three times a day, will help. Cut down on its intake of fat. Lean meat, skimmed milk, and brown bread will help, I think.